# MY JAMAICAN FATHER

## A True Story

*by*

Julie Wood

Grosvenor House
Publishing Limited

This book is published by
Grosvenor House Publishing Ltd
Link House
140 The Broadway, Tolworth, Surrey, KT6 7HT.
www.grosvenorhousepublishing.co.uk

A CIP record for this book
is available from the British Library

ISBN 978-1-83615-235-4

*Written for my daughters*

*Katie    Trudy    and    Lizzie*

# Chapter One

My father was born on a beautiful Caribbean island of Jamaica. It was 1922. His own father was called Cecil Augustas Tait. The locals called him Custas. Cecil had a very jovial look about him. Fine features, with dark complexion. His eyes were smiling and bright and seemed pleased with his lot. His face was round and jolly, sporting a 'handlebar' moustache above his upper lip. It was an extremely wide moustache—and exaggerated. It must have been the fashion on the island at the time. In fact, Cecil looked a bit of a dandy type of a person, I would go as far to say. Very good looking and well presented. A look of mischievousness in his smile. I would say my father took the look of his father: that round-faced, jovial, happy look.

The name of my father's mother was Ethel, known as Sis. Her maiden name was Sanguinetti, an Italian name. I remember, as a child, seeing a photograph of the two of them secreted away under my mother's hat collection in the wardrobe. It was a black and white photo—as there was no colour in those days. I seem to remember Ethel's face being long and thin. It was an unsmiling, matter-of-fact sort of face, in a natural pose. Ethel was neither beautiful, nor was she plain. She had Mediterranean looks with an olive complexion and shoulder-length straight black hair. I can still see the photo now, ingrained in my mind. A snapshot, available to be seen whenever the feeling takes me.

My father lived in a place called Bamboo. It was situated high up on a hilltop, in the parish of Saint Ann. The road up the steep hill is now properly made with tarmac. It becomes winding with unmade roads leading off to other people's properties. About halfway up the hill, there is a viewpoint, where you can rest and admire the scenery for miles and miles. It's such a steep incline all the way up to where the house is. From the road, you can see the house where my father lived. An unmade track leading to the property.

Apparently, Cecil had built the house himself, with the help of local friends and neighbours. They would all go to the nearby wood to chop down trees. The trees were hardwood, mahogany. I can imagine the scene. All the women would make up their fires outside among the trees. They would set up huge pots of curried goat and rice and peas, Jamaica's national food. When the work was done, they would all gather round to eat. I visited the house when I went to Jamaica in the year 2006. We, the British, would call it a bungalow. Steps led up to a veranda, leading through to the inside of the property. The house itself was basic. Quite a few rooms though, with a kitchen on the back dropping down to very steep steps, into the back yard.

The people, in those days, were very convivial and friendly. Most families had their own family homesteads. When somebody was travelling from afar and needed a place to rest their weary head, people would be happy to offer respite for the night. Being a Christian community, they would always help their fellow man.

My father's house had a great deal of land attached to it. They would grow vegetables and plant trees. By nature, they were farmers who lived off the land and took produce to the local market in Saint Ann, to sell, or barter. Banana, breadfruit, ackee, tangerine and jackfruit trees, were grown, together with coffee bushes. Cabbages, sweet potato, Irish potatoes (the white English type were called Irish potatoes) were grown abundantly on the acres of land. Neighbours would barter their produce with each other. When a man went down to the sea to do some fishing, he would bring the fish back home, take what he needed, then swap the rest with a neighbour for, say, some tangerines or breadfruit.

There was no idea of shops in those days. You lived off the land. Things like refined sugar would be bought in Saint Ann's market. It was weighed by the bushel (a measure of weight, like ounces, pounds and kilos) and would be carried home in your own container.

There were animals, such as pigs, goats and chickens all housed on the land. A pig would be slaughtered, the meat salted and stored underneath the back of the house, for later use. If a chicken was needed for dinner, the man of the house would take it and wring its neck to kill the poor unfortunate creature. The head would be chopped off with a machete, simple as that, no messing about. The machete was a basic tool needed for everyday living and was kept very sharp—very sharp indeed.

Life was simple. Cecil would take his donkey and ride to the furthest part of his land to cultivate the crops. This became his life. Every day, he would take a bit of food, like a chunk of cooked pork meat and breadfruit, maybe a tangerine or two, and a drink of water. I suppose you are asking yourself, water? Where did water come from? Well, remember, the climate in Jamaica could become extreme. There was the hurricane season, for example. When it rained and rained, the water came down from the sky in torrents, loads of it. Water barrels were placed at various points under the roof of the house for the rainwater to be collected and stored. If the water became too much for the barrel, it was transferred to a main tank further down the land. So on and so forth, the collection went on.

When my father talked about his childhood, he would say that he always had to check himself before he ventured out of the house. Let me explain this bit. In Jamaica, very often an argument or altercation would break out in the neighbourhood. People would rush out of their homes to see what was going on, somebody injured needing help or whatever. A crowd of people would gather. You must remember, there was very little in the way of entertainment in those days. In such circumstances, his mother always told him to look into the mirror to check whether his face was dirty or whether his hair wasn't right, to check himself, before he ran out. Can you imagine the frustration of my father wanting to see what was going on, always having to stop first to look into a mirror... wow! Discipline dished out alright...

# Chapter Two

Before they had married, Ethel had lived in Kingston. Apparently, she came from Kingston with a child she had named Samuel. He was born in 1913. On reaching the parish of Saint Ann, she had found work in a Great House as a housekeeper. The owner of the house had a son called Hardcastle. She had got together with Hardcastle, and bore him a child, whom she named Claude. Claude was white like his father. He grew to be tall and skinny. Apparently, Hardcastle always acknowledged his illegitimate child. Later on in life, he got to know him much better and treated him as one of his family. Now later, Ethel gave birth to a baby girl. I do not know who the father was. She named her Muriel—who later changed her own name to Claudette.

So, Ethel already had three of her own children before she married Cecil Tait. The children born to them were my father, Emmett, then Monica, Delphina, Pearl, Hyacinth, Phyllis, Beresford and Dita. (Delphina passed away as a child; I do not know the circumstances.) My father was the first-born child in the marriage, the eldest. He was affectionately known as 'Babes'. For years, everybody in the family, friends and neighbours always referred to him as by that name.

It was a simple life as a child growing up. My father would arise out of his bed in the morning, run over to his grandmother's (Minnie Scarlett) house to fetch the milk. She was the only person in the family who owned a cow. Then he would go to school, which was situated at the bottom of the steep hill in Bamboo. The year was about 1927.

The school did not have many textbooks. Being a small island, any books they had were old and worn. The children were given a slate to write on. Each boy and girl was given a piece of chalk to write with.

The children at the school were encouraged to speak the King's English, without sloppiness. Pronounce your h's and cross your t's was instilled into the students. Jamaica, after all, was a commonwealth country, ruled by the British. The history taught in the school was British history. My father was taught to remember dates like the Battle of Hastings, 1066. He listened to stories about English Kings and Queens. They learned the history of the Anglo Saxons, Medieval England and the Victorian age.

In Geography lessons, children studied large English cities like London, Leeds, Manchester and Birmingham. They navigated maps of the British Isles, discovering different regions. English poetry was recited. Reading British magazines and newspaper articles was common and quite natural. The same was being taught in British schools all the way over in England, the 'Mother Country'. Most Jamaicans thought this was the proper way to be and live like the English. The fast-speaking Patois was discouraged. It was frowned upon.

The schoolteachers were very strict. You weren't allowed to talk, especially when the teacher was talking. When a child spoke out of turn or answered back to the teacher, they were given 'a good thrashing' by him or her. Then, after school, the teacher would go to your home, where you lived, to tell your parents all about what had happened. When the teacher left, you would then get another thrashing from your parents. Also, over in England, the school children's punishment was the cane. My father told me, he never ever got a thrashing... Smile... It was indeed zero tolerance to bad behaviour.

My father told me about an incident where he was being bullied by another boy. Day after day, the boy would say horrible things to him, relentlessly. One day, my father finally snapped. He could not listen to the boy's comments any longer. So, on his way home, as the boy was there yet again saying nasty things to him, Dad grabbed him, then started thumping him and eventually beat this boy up really badly. My dad totally and completely lost his temper. The older boys had to intervene to separate them. From that day on, the boy would always avoid him, wherever he went!

On a Caribbean island, the daylight starts to falter as early as six o'clock in the evening. In the 1920s, there was very little to occupy oneself after darkness fell. Oil lamps were lit to give a bit of light. I suppose people would just retire to their beds. So you could say the people were well rested!

On the occasion of someone's birthday, or Christmastime, it would be celebrated with the absence of gifts. People would attend their local church to praise the Lord. This was the tradition.

# Chapter Three

Ethel Sanguinetti's mother, Minnie Scarlett, lived a few fields away from Ethel's house. (She was the lady with the cow—well, I do not know anything about Mr Sanguinetti.) My dad understood the name to be Portuguese. He was told his mother was of Portuguese descent, as a child, but the name actually stems from Italy originally. A bit of a grey area here.

Whether she had been married to him and perhaps he later died, or whatever, I do not know very much about the history of her. My father told me that she was very light-skinned. She was small in stature and very smiley faced. Her son was called Frank, who had joined the merchant navy during the First World War. He would send money over to her, as this is what most boys did at the time. Apparently, his ship was torpedoed, and word came about that he had been killed.

When my father talked about Minnie, his grandmother, he smiled easily and said she was always kind to him. She had called him Babes. My father had told me that he really loved her and he actually called her 'Mum'. Of course, he would see her every morning when he ran over to her house to fetch the milk. And he would often go to play at his grandmother's house with the other children. When she offered him some refreshment, he would always refuse. She used to get quite upset about this state of affairs. One day, she mentioned this to his mother and his mother gave him a good telling off for being so rude and impolite.

My father was around 13 years of age when Minnie Scarlett unfortunately lost her sight. She became blind. Her blindness must have been so tragic for her, for she coped very well. Even so, Minnie went on to live until she was a hundred years old.

Ethel had a sister called Muriel. She was a small woman in height. Her personality was vibrant and sunny. She married a man called Mr Rumble. Children came along. A boy called Levi was born and grew up, my dad's cousin, obviously. My father hung around with Levi and they were good friends. Levi lived to be eighty-nine years old.

# Chapter Four

Cecil Tait, known as Custas, as I have described in a previous chapter, was a very upbeat, jolly type of person. He was a farmer who worked the land. Interestingly though, whenever there was a rock fall in the neighbourhood, they would send for Custas. Especially in the hurricane season, the roads could become quite hazardous. The torrents of rain would bring down rocks, which would be strewn all over the road, thus blocking it. Custas was the explosives expert. Maybe he had spent some time working in the bauxite mine earlier in his life. This could explain how he became knowledgeable. He would always be called to set a charge among the rocks. A large boulder that blocked the road would be blown to smithereens. Then they could clear the road more easily. Even further down the road in Saint Ann, if there was any blockage of the road, they would say, 'Send for Custas!'—for Custas had the know-how—and they would call for him.

Also, Custas used to keep honey bees. On his land he had constructed a hive or two. There was no special equipment like there is nowadays. My father remembers him using smoke to make the bees docile. He would then collect the honey. Later, he would scrape off the wax, which would be used to polish the mahogany floors inside the house.

Remember Custas had built his own house, which his family lived in. This must have been at the turn of the century, say 1900, give or take a few years. Now Custas had an abundance of brothers and sisters. Connie, Reginald, Victor, Ernest, Cissie, Dassy, Tartar and Winnie. I know Dassy later came over to England to reside and she lived to be one hundred years old.

Reginald went to work in the prison in Saint Ann, called Hill Top Prison. He was a prison warden. They say he was a bit too keen on keeping the prisoners in line. He meted out the discipline a bit too mean and harsh. He wouldn't let them smoke cigarettes in certain areas, for example. Other prison wardens were a bit more relaxed, and the rules were a bit more laid back, but not Reginald. He was strict and the prisoners grew to dislike him immensely. One night, a prisoner just couldn't take the harsh treatment from Reginald. The story goes that he got chopped up and killed with a machete. Yes, they killed the poor guy. God rest his soul. How absolutely tragic for his family. He was forty-four years old.

Another brother, Victor, was a bit of a mystery. He travelled over to Cuba and stayed there for most of his days. We do not know whether he had married or whatever. Apparently, he ventured back to Jamaica when Cecil passed away. (This was in the early 1960s.) Cecil had just collapsed and died while working in the fields. His wife, Ethel, so overcome by grief, passed away within a year. So Victor came back to Jamaica solely to claim his brother's land, trying to take advantage of the young daughters' lack of knowledge.

Now it was Cecil's daughters who were left to sort out their father's estate. Traditionally in Jamaica, it is all left to the eldest son, who was my father. In fact, when my father later found himself living in England, they sent important documents over to him to sign the family home and land over to his sister Pearl. I know that in the family Victor had been painted as the bad guy, for he only returned to Jamaica to try to claim part of the land. I really do not know the ins and outs of the saga, but he caused a bit of disruption in the family. He later disappeared back to Cuba.

There was a family member called Bridgett M. Webb. My father told me that she was the wild one in the family. Dad had called her Aunty B. She had children with different men, which wasn't really that unusual on the island of Jamaica at the time. My father didn't really expand on her antics, but just said 'she was a bit wild' and laughed. She didn't run her life the way the other Taits did. For the family were churchgoing Methodists. Family members later held jobs which were regarded as professional and law abiding. What was said about the Taits, is that they 'never put a foot wrong'...

Cecil's brother Ernest had a lawyer type of mentality. When anyone in the neighbourhood had a grievance, Ernest would become involved, in an impartial way. He would listen to both sides of the story, then he would suggest they talk it out. All persons would say what they wanted to say, then they would all come to a peaceful solution about what to do next. Ernest would be a bystander in an advisory capacity. Any altercation in Bamboo and they would say, 'Send for Ernest!'

# Chapter Five

The date was on or around the sixteenth of August 1922 when my father was born. At the time, a lot of births were just written into the back of the family Bible as a record. Officialdom did not really exist much, as it is today. Even so, it seems Cecil actually went to the register office in Spanish Town, *in person*, to register the birth. The birth certificate shows my father's name as Samuel Joseph. The 'Emmett' is traditionally added on as a baptismal name—a further name added at the baptism of a child. So, my father is known as Emmett Samuel Joseph Tait.

When a child is born, the tradition is that the umbilical cord is taken. A hole in the ground is dug. The cord is put into the hole, then a breadfruit tree is planted. The superstition is, whatever height the tree grows, the longer the child shall live. When I visited Jamaica in the year 2006, I found my father's breadfruit tree. I looked up at it and could not see the top. It was bushy, huge, healthy and high!

As you can imagine, it is very hot in Jamaica, but in Bamboo, where it is higher up, the air is a little cooler with breezes gently caressing the vegetation. There is a huge variety of vegetation. The breadfruit trees, banana and tangerine trees had fed the family for years.

Tangerines, just picked fresh off the tree, have a green skin and the flesh is an orange colour. This is because in hot countries, the green chlorophyll is preserved and the outside of the fruit stays green, which is when they can be picked and eaten. It is when the temperature changes, like when they are shipped off to England or other countries, the skin changes to an orange colour.

# Chapter Six

On the third of September 1939, Sir Neville Chamberlain, prime minister of England, broadcast a radio announcement. War had been declared. England was at war with Germany. The radio announcement reverberated around the world. There was a sense of excitement in Jamaica when my father and his family heard. In those days, England was known as the Mother Country to most West Indian islands—England and the British monarch ruled the island of Jamaica and many others. His Majesty, King George VI, was Jamaica's figurehead too.

A year later, Chamberlain began to have health issues. He had to resign and Winston Churchill took over from him as prime minister. At this time, the British Government decided to recruit people into the British military from Empire countries, to help out in the war. But it would not allow Caribbean people to join the British Armed Forces. It had been noted that Winston Churchill was dubious about black men serving alongside white men on equal terms. There were English business men living in Jamaica at the time who were concerned about this. They wanted the locals to contribute to the war. They decided to prove Churchill was wrong. So, they set about funding a trip themselves and sent a group of young Jamaicans to England as volunteers to the Royal Air Force camp.

It was proved they could easily do the work of fellow British military men and they were bright-minded, hard-working young people. So, the Colonial Office changed their minds. They decided to recruit Jamaicans and small island people into the British RAF. Over a few years, five thousand Caribbean men and women were recruited.

Now local Jamaican leaders weren't happy about their fellow men going off to 'fight'. They did not want them to be used on the front line of battle. Also, it was England's war with Germany, not Jamaicans' war with the Germans. An agreement was made. Jamaican recruits would only help them out from a supportive capacity. So this was better news for the Jamaican young men and women.

Now, there was a drinking bar just down the road where Cecil would take my dad to chat, meet friends and while away the time. A notice was put up by the British RAF officers. It was about wanting to recruit local Jamaicans, to join the war. Also, there was a promise made for them to be able to learn a trade when, eventually, the war would be over. My father was aged about twenty years old. There wasn't much work to be had for young men on the island at this time. Many of my dad's friends thought this was a huge opportunity to leave the island by joining up to help in the war, for there were very few prospects in Jamaica.

Cecil didn't say much about it. He just said to Dad something like, 'It's up to you son.' So Dad filled in the application form, which later meant he had to take a written test because not just anybody could be recruited—they had to have a certain amount of intelligence. The application form was posted off, along with many others. They had to wait and wait...

At first, my dad didn't hear from the RAF for months on end. Cecil often travelled to Kingston town and had formed contacts in various shops. He told Dad that there was a bit of work available in a haberdashery shop. It was owned by an African Assyrian man, who apparently had a beautiful wife. The shop was in a wealthy neighbourhood just down from

Saint Andrew. Dad travelled to Kingston and was given work as a gardener initially in exchange for board and lodgings and a little bit of money. The labouring didn't last long because of the economy on the island. Businesses were slowly falling into decline, so the Assyrian had to serve notice on my father and the work was lost. He tried to search around for more work, but there was nothing much available. Dad would not have any dinner for days on end, only managing to scrounge a few crusts of bread here and there.

At this time a young upstart called Alexander Bustamante was rebel rousing in Kingston, Jamaica. He spread the word to newspapers about the poverty and hardship that people faced. Children wore rags in the street, for they had no clothes to wear. There was extreme hunger too. The banana trade had drastically declined and unemployment was high. The bananas were inflicted with Panama disease, which destroyed crops.

There was only occasional work. Bad nutrition, poor housing, very little health service and the cost of living was high. Bustamante started a strike with the men working on Kingston docks. They wanted to work for better wages and the unemployed joined the strike demanding work.

I quote part of a letter from Alexander Bustamante written to the Editor, *Daily Gleaner*, Kingston:

> *The mongoose and the rats in certain parts of the island are being disturbed at nights, because the cane fields, their resting places, have now become the sleeping place of many workers. Many of them rush out at nights so nude they dare not come out in the days, just to buy little necessities to return to their shelter – the cane fields.*
>
> *I have been to Saint Ann and the poverty there is something I hate to describe. Neither minister or*

*politician should try to prevent it being exposed. Visit Newton, Kinowl, Mullings, Bush Districts in Saint Elizabeth, Marlie Hill and Plowden and see the poverty – the misery...' too late it is for anyone through any peculiar reasons to try and cover up the truth of the lamentable conditions. Things were bad a few years gone by, they were no better last year, this year they are getting worse, there must be better days ahead.*

*I am etc.*

*Alexander Bustamante*

Things were so bad, Dad decided to hitch a lift back home to Bamboo, Saint Ann. His folks in Bamboo had lived off the land. They grew their own vegetables and kept a menagerie of goats and chickens, so at least he would be able to eat at home. He walked along the coast road and thumbed a ride from any passing truck that happened to come along. A donkey with cart came by and the owner was glad to give some respite to the tired traveller.

The hot sun beaming down made Dad very thirsty. On the last haul of the journey back home, the steep hill from the coast road was too much. He apparently came upon some water in an oil drum container at the side of the road. Dad, so thirsty, scooped the refreshing water from the drum. It must have seemed like heaven to him. Little did he know that this water was contaminated. On reaching home in Bamboo, family and friends were glad to see him but were concerned at his demeanour. Dad fell to the floor and became seriously ill. His father, Cecil, picked him up and placed him in his bed.

For days and nights, he developed a fever and became delirious. There was no local GP or doctor in those days. His father became so worried that he summoned the herb doctor. Concoctions were boiled up and dispensed to my father, but to no avail. They thought he would die. On around the fifth day, my dad tentatively took to his feet. He was very, very weak. He mustered up all of his strength and walked outside to a tree. He had remembered the bark of this tree had some medicinal properties. So, with a knife, he cut off some of the bark. Back in the house he boiled it up in a pan set on the stove. When the mixture was cool, he drank it and went back to his bed. That night, the fever suddenly left him. And Dad recovered against all odds.

A while later, a letter arrived from the RAF. Dad was to take a test for the recruitment. There was very little choice for him but to go ahead. A lot of young men and women in the neighbourhood had joined him. Some fathers did not want their sons and daughters to go. There was fear that they would never see them again. But what were the young people supposed to do? Migration was the only answer. Some young men and women did stay at home with their families for fear of the unknown.

My father had passed his test and was asked to go down to the British barracks in Kingston. They were taking a truck load down the following week. So this was it! My father was going to leave the island and join the RAF.

On the morning of the departure, he had called for his friend Lester. Lester answered the door and said, 'I am not going. My father does not want me to go.' So, a bit dismayed and disappointed, my dad said his goodbyes and joined the others waiting down the road.

They all walked to Saint Ann where they were loaded onto a military truck which took them to Kingston. My father's pioneering journey had begun. Rumour has it, there was a girlfriend tearfully waving 'goodbye', begging him not to go…

# Chapter Seven

Dad and many others were summoned to take another test on arrival. This time it was a medical test. They all arrived at a hall designated for the recruitment. They were to be examined and medically tested by doctors and nurses. Dad checked out alright, but a friend of his didn't have very good eyesight so was a bit worried about getting through the examination. When the friend walked into the room, there was apparently a Jamaican assistant, whom he recognised as his old playmate back in the Parish. The assistant was there to make notes during the eye test. When it came to the man's sight problems, the assistant looked at him, smiled and nodded, then passed him through... A stroke of luck for this young man!

The Jamaicans were taken to a camp in Kingston called Palisadoes. This is now called Norman Manley Airport. It was a large central place where men and women from all over the Caribbean were grouped together. Men and women were kitted out with RAF uniforms, rucksacks, boots—but no rifles or guns.

The young Jamaicans were not a very disciplined bunch of people. They really didn't know the military jargon; obviously, they were new to it all. My dad lined up on parade. There was a lot of noisy chatter. The strict discipline of the British military seemed to be an ordeal for the new recruits. There was misunderstanding from the Caribbean people. The officers shouted their commands loudly. The men and women thought they were being rude to them and downright disrespectful with all the shouting. They didn't understand how it all worked and were wondering why those British officers were shouting at them. Had they done something wrong? So they retaliated. 'Why are you shouting at us?'

They started to become unsettled from the way they were being treated. Soon the officers realised they needed to sit them down, to explain that 'orders' given to them were in fact always 'shouted' and not spoken... Ha ha. It must have seemed quite comical at the time—as an onlooker.

So, having to accept their new way of life, the recruits endured their training in the camp. They understood how to march, how to look after their uniforms and kit. The discipline was dished out and my dad took to it like a duck to water, and enjoyed it!

The food in the camp was not like the food their families served at home. The vegetables were boiled in water and didn't taste very good. The meals were downright bland. The men and women weren't very happy about this situation. They had never tasted cabbage, nor carrots. The food they ate at home was spicy and they fried their vegetables rather than boiled them. But my dad was happy to have three meals a day. The food was plentiful. They all could not believe the amount of food given to them and really enjoyed it. Dad certainly felt things were looking up for him.

The training was gruelling. Every day, in the hot heat of Jamaica, they marched up hills and down hills for miles; this was in full uniform and extremely tiring. They marched in small groups and paraded around parts of Kingston. Hundreds of people turned out to wish them well. Groups of new recruits frequented the cinema. Apparently, there was a Bing Crosby film showing called *Holiday Inn*. There were great crowds gathering in the streets of Kingston. People knew the men and women in uniform were going to be sailing off to join the war.

Back at the barracks, things were kept quiet. The Caribbean people did not know when to expect to be boarding their ship bound for England. Men and women slept in their full uniforms as they were told to. There were night drills where they would be woken at three o'clock in the morning and ordered out onto the parade ground for roll call, then ordered back to bed again.

Usually, the lights would go out at nine thirty and they would retire for the evening. Then, in the early hours of the morning, again, they were ordered out of their beds. Already dressed in uniform, they marched and paraded around the barracks and their rucksacks would be put on board a military truck as if they were leaving. There was a feeling of expectation in the air. Then wham! After all that, they would be ordered back to bed! The rucksacks would be returned also. This was always happening—for weeks on end. These false alarms were frequent. People were moaning about this and some were getting sick and tired of the now routine. The sleep disruption became tiring.

The time of their departure had to be kept top secret. Remember, this was war time and nobody could know exactly when they would be leaving the island. This was a full-scale military operation. Because of the war, troop ships needed to be accompanied and convoys were put into position in the Atlantic Ocean.

Submarines, destroyers, frigates had to be put in place all over the route the troop ships would eventually take. When the night came to prepare to set sail, my dad and others couldn't believe how quickly it all took place. All men and women were, as usual, ordered to arise from their beds in the small hours of the morning. Boots on. The rucksacks were put on board the waiting truck. But this time, the instructions from the British commanding officer were different. The men and women were ordered to remove their boots and carry them, not to talk and to walk quietly.

So, picture the scene: RAF new recruits, a long line of them walking the streets. Along the route, some locals opened their windows and looked out to see what was going on. I suppose this couldn't be helped. The local people knew what was happening and realised the time had come for them to board ship.

When my dad and all of them arrived at the dock, they quietly boarded and set sail, bound for England. It was indeed a very smooth and quick operation...

# Chapter Eight

My dad travelled with a convoy of Jamaican and small island recruits. They were aboard a ship called the SS *Cuba*. It was the summer of 1944. The ship was protected by two American destroyers. They were heading for Virginia in the USA, a place called Camp Patrick Henry, Newport News, Virginia. There was to be some reorganisation of ships. The RAF men and women were told not to have any sexual relations, with the locals, for fear of catching venereal disease. The orders were that any man or woman who caught such an illness would be sent home. So, being sent home like this would have been quite embarrassing.

The Americans had been known, at the time, to disrespect their own black people, so it was puzzling the Jamaicans and small island people were greeted well by American men and women. Indeed, made a friendly fuss of. I suspect this was because Jamaica was in the British Empire ruled by King George VI, thus thought of and accepted as British. They treated them like guests and were friendly and when off duty, the new recruits were invited to social events like dance parties. For example, while the American black men and women stood outside the dance halls, ostracised by the white American soldiers, the black Jamaicans were inside the dance hall having a really good time.

There were a lot of ships to be organised by the military. The ships bound for England had to be escorted. Ships like destroyers, frigates and corvettes had to be put into place before they could carry on the rest of the journey. So after about two weeks, Dad and his fellow troops set sail again. They had changed ship. This time the troops were reassigned to the HMT *Harrower* (HMT meaning His Majesty's Trawler). The *Harrower* was a New Zealand ship and the ship had to be shared with New Zealand troops also.

So, my dad, on board the *Harrower*, was heading now for Newfoundland. The seas were high and very rough. It was a terrible crossing apparently. When passing Newfoundland and on target for England, Dad and his fellow men became very frightened. The high seas were hurling the *Harrower* up and down. Rolling, rollicking, rough. At times, the ship reached angles of 60 degrees, crashing and banging through the waves. They feared the ship would turn over and sink. Troops were terribly seasick. A lot of the Jamaicans were wishing they were back home. Some really thought they would never survive. Young men cried in fear for their lives.

Nearing England, early in the morning, my father woke up to really calm seas. A formation of battleships, destroyers, corvettes, frigates and cruise ships were surrounding the *Harrower*. All troops breathed a sigh of relief. They must have felt so safe and protected. Such a sight to see, this lovely convoy...

On the sea, the HMT *Harrower* travelled down Britain's north coastline. Two ports were used, Liverpool and Greenock. My dad and his friends docked in Liverpool. It was lovely, the landing. As they disembarked, a band was assembled at the dockside, playing the latest songs. The greeting party was fabulous. Even a high-ranking officer, the Right Honourable Colonel Oliver Stanley MP was there to receive them.

A huge crowd of English military women were present, making cups of coffee and tea. They were very friendly and became excitable, in their banter.

They made the troops feel most welcome with their infectious exuberance. The young women were very animated and told jokes. Groups of women were singing. This made them feel at home. For although it was an English summer, it was warm, but could not compare with the heat of the Caribbean. The new recruits complained of the 'cool' weather. So, they were given military coats to wear.

# Chapter Nine

After the greeting celebrations, Dad and the troops marched quickly to the train station. They would be travelling to a place called Hunmanby Moor in Filey, Yorkshire. From there, they would march to Butlins Holiday Camp, which was now being used by the RAF. The journey would take about fifteen hours. They were transported by steam train. There were English women working at the train station, handling heavy suitcases and bags, which the young recruits found astonishing. Dad talked to me about the general atmosphere in the carriages: 'Most people were in high spirits. We all talked about our homes and wondered what our families would be doing at this very moment…'

The servicemen and women admired the green of the countryside and the formality of the hedging. The fields and hedgerows seemed neat and tidy, with hedges seemingly separating the landscape. The English countryside was breathtakingly beautiful. England was just how they had imagined. They recalled the pictures from the books and magazines they had seen back home. Most of them fell asleep from the motion of the train.

Along the journey, there were women working in the fields and driving heavy tractors. They also drove trucks and army vehicles. Dad and his friends were amazed at how these English women worked so hard, for at home, this would never happen; the men, only, would do this kind of work. It seemed unbelievable to the men and women. But most of the young and able-bodied English men had gone off to fight for the country, so somebody had to do the work.

On the way to Hunmanby Moor, the train stopped at small towns. The young men pushed down their windows to chat to the young girls waiting on the platform. People were amiable. Friendly banter took place. Cigarettes were swapped for sweets and biscuits. The West Indians were surprised at the scarcity of these items, for these supplies had been plentiful back at the camp in Kingston. The rationing in Britain was more severe.

This was war time. Suddenly the train was immersed into darkness. The young people began to panic, for they had never experienced a tunnel before. Some screamed and thought they were being attacked. They emerged out of the tunnel unharmed! At night-time, the train windows had to be covered so as not to expose the lights of the train.

Finally, the train arrived at Hunmanby Moor station. It seemed a quiet and desolate place. The Caribbean people disembarked and began their march through the streets.

Curtains were twitching from nearby houses. Local people had never seen black people before. Now, there were hundreds marching. Local people came out of their houses to watch. Children were holding onto their mothers and seemed afraid. My father sensed they were being checked out by the white people; one child was seen looking at the backsides of the black men to see whether they indeed had a tail like a monkey. They had heard different descriptions of black people, for the English, at this time, were ignorant. They had very little knowledge. Indeed, they had probably only seen pictures in books and magazines, but not actually seen any in the flesh. So, of course the people were inquisitive—especially in a small sleepy seaside village.

# Chapter Ten

The camp at Filey had been built in 1939, the first English holiday camp of its kind. From 1939–1945, it was used as a military training base and was called RAF Hunmanby Moor. This was my dad's first home in England, the Mother Country. The camp was situated on top of a cliff. The views across the sea and surrounding countryside were awe-inspiring. There were green fields and country lanes all around. From the camp, after a short walk, there were roughly made steps leading to the beach. The lilting sound of the waves crashing on the beach at night must have been very soothing. It was a peaceful environment.

The buildings themselves were comfortable but became cold in the autumn and winter. Because they were initially built for use in the summer months, there was very little in the way of heating. Dad and his fellow men complained of bitterly cold mornings. The only form of heating was the hot pipes situated just above the skirting board. When the winter months came, Dad described the frozen ice on the inside of the windows. When they came to open an outside door, they couldn't because it was all frozen up. So they used their bayonets to chip away the ice.

The dining halls were absolutely immaculate. White tablecloths were crisply starched. The glasses twinkled in the light, with gleaming cutlery in abundance. Everything was set out exact and clean as a new pin.

Dad remembers meals like roast beef and Yorkshire pudding served with all the greens and trimmings. He could eat as much as he wanted, then was given an apple for dessert. The servicemen and women were well fed. Some troops complained though. They said the food was not spicy enough. So later on, the menu was changed—when they had appointed a Caribbean cook. My father never expected to be treated so well! For he had only seen white tablecloths and china at expensive restaurants and hotels in Kingston, Jamaica. He was well pleased and grateful. Indeed, they all were.

Every day they had to rise from their billets early. The men and women were trained how to handle handguns, rifles and bayonets. They were exercised by taking part in cross-country runs. They practised square-bashing on the camp with and without weapons. Discipline was drilled into them. Styles of marching were practised. Classroom lessons were given on how to identify enemy aircraft and to distinguish German planes from British. They took part in unarmed combat also.

On completion of military training, each was to be given an assessment exam. These were known as trade tests. It would identify servicemen capabilities and would determine which job or trade was given to whom. Dad told me he took a series of tests. There were different types of aptitude tests, which fell broadly into three categories. Those who passed with higher marks in English and Maths were given jobs in clerical, administration, pay and accounts. The low scorers became general dogsbodies as aircraft hands carrying out general duties. There was also a set of mechanical tests and those who scored high found themselves being designated to radar, wireless operating, and flight mechanic trades. My father's trade was found to be clerical.

The Jamaicans knew before they signed up they would learn a trade and would be assigned apprenticeships. This was a good incentive to join the RAF in the first place. When the war was over, they would have gained a qualification and would be able to use it to find employment out of the RAF. Some had even informed senior officers of their views about which trades they would like to study for: truck mechanic or radio expert etc. Well, it came to pass that they received bad news. Their flight lieutenant announced their original chosen trades had to be rejigged. It was now not possible to choose what they had wanted. This caused a lot of resentment with the servicemen. Some even wondered whether to go back home. They felt they had been recruited under false pretences.

However, my father settled into the clerical/ administration trade and was satisfied. The life was good. He easily settled into military life and became contented. For entertainment, the service people were allowed to venture into the nearby village of Hunmanby or Filey town in the evenings.

On a Saturday night, dances were held at the Hunmanby Institute. They charged one shilling entrance fee. Local RAF people were welcome and girls came from Filey, Muston, North Burton and Reighton etc. The servicemen and women would be loaded onto a troop truck and were taken to wherever they wanted to go for the evening. Some wandered into local pubs. They had never experienced pubs before.

In the daytime, they visited local shops to buy stuff. But, to their dismay, they couldn't find half of what they needed because of the rationing. Elderly people would visit the camp at Filey and invited Jamaican and small island men and women to their houses for tea. They wanted to know more about their new black neighbours.

# Chapter Eleven

After my father's basic training, the camp servicemen and women were dispersed to other camps down to the south of Britain. My father's next stop was RAF Melksham. So when the Filey camp was empty of military personnel, another set of new Caribbean recruits came along to replace them.

RAF Melksham was specially built in early 1940. Melksham is a southern English village near Chippenham and Trowbridge, situated near Bath/ Bristol area. In July, the RAF School of Instrument Training moved here from RAF Cranwell. Specialist training took place for ground crew. There was no runway. The war planes were brought in on lorries in a dismantled state. This was so the trainees could put them back together again. Melksham, at this time, hosted a mixture of nationalities. They included the Polish and the Free French airmen. The American camps were based nearby.

They would learn all the technicalities of different types of war planes, like the Hurricane, the Halifax, the Lancaster and the Wellingtons. The official title of the station was No. 12 School of Technical Training. Local people would find aircraft on display, but the planes would not fly from Melksham.

In the daytime, the men and women trained hard. In the evening, they would walk to the local pubs and cinemas, or stay at the camp to read and study. The camps had a place called the NAAFI (the Navy, Army and Air Force Institute). It was like a social club. When the NAAFI organised a dance, usually on a weekend, most military personnel would want to attend from all the camps.

The tables had turned and the white Americans had changed their view of the Jamaicans and small island black people. The British personnel, the Jamaicans, small island people, black Americans, would all attend and be dancing together under one roof. And, well, there were a lot of altercations, and fights broke out as a consequence.

My father recalls one particular occasion. There was going to be a Christmas Eve dance at the NAAFI. Now, the white Americans did not like the white women dancing with the black Caribbeans. The white American airmen had told their own women (WAAFs) to avoid the black airmen and specifically not to dance with them.

There obviously now was a very tense atmosphere. The word got around the camp about what the Americans had told their girls. The only WAAFs going would be with their boyfriends. So, just to show off and upset their plans, the West Indians trucked in a load of local girls. (A week before the dance, they had set off to nearby villages and invited them.) On the evening, hundreds of local girls turned up to the dance party. Of course, they danced with the black men! And the white airmen were absolutely furious.

Fights broke out at the dance. A white airman would go up to a black airman and cause trouble. They would deliberately knock their drinks over or say nasty words to them. Of course, the black men would not stand for this kind of hassle and a terrible fight blew up. Remember, they were all young men with the hot heads of youth.

The whole of the NAAFI club was completely and utterly destroyed. All the bottles and drinks were smashed to pieces.

Some men pulled out knives and became threatening. Fortunately, no one actually died, which was a miracle. There were almost twice as many Americans to Jamaicans and islanders, so the black men were badly beaten up.

As a result of this, the next day, their commanding officer was furious. He summoned the Caribbean men and women to take part in a meeting and tried to find out of who had started the fighting. He was absolutely 'out of his mind' with rage. He started to accuse certain people of things they hadn't done or said. Some of the Jamaicans started to answer back. Some began to swear at him, which wasn't the correct thing to do to a higher officer (the commanding officer being white British). There was a complete breakdown of discipline and morals.

Usually, it would be a chargeable offence to disrespect your commanding officer. The boys were really upset and angry. Some spoke their native patois. There was a lot of shouting and abusive language hurled at the officer. (Of course, this was also Christmas Day.) In the end, the meeting broke down and the commanding officer just walked out in disgust.

From the point of view of the RAF, it seemed it was going to be a lot of hard work and quite difficult to find out exactly which men were the culprits who had instigated the bust-ups. So what the British commanding officers decided to do was banish them and send them all away to an isolated camp just outside Lincolnshire. The place was called Strubby near Alford in Lincolnshire. They packed all of the Caribbean people into a troop truck and took them away.

Strubby was a disused aerodrome. It was like a sub camp with a few buildings and a runway. The camp ethos was very relaxed with only the one commanding officer in charge. Things were a bit too slack. For example, when a man was punished, he wasn't supposed to go out of the camp but be looked after by the officer in charge. Later, the two men would be seen drinking in the local pub.

The camp was out in the sticks, very boring with very little to do. The men and women were given bikes so they could ride to nearby villages in the evening. Sometimes, when there was a dance on in Mablethorpe, which was seven miles away, a whole load of men and women would be going together. A huge troop truck was given to them and a driver would be assigned to take charge and drive them to the dance and bring them back home later. The men could also cycle or be trucked to Mablethorpe for six o'clock, the time when the pubs would open their doors.

Even so, internally there were still a lot of misunderstandings and altercations. Jamaicans argued among themselves, accusing each other of arrogance and rudeness. The Trinidadians, Kittitians and Ghanaians thought the Jamaicans were a bunch of 'show-offs'. They would often fall out and start fights. Being young men and women, they were opinionated and found it difficult to control their tempers.

# Chapter Twelve

Double summertime was introduced to Britain in 1942 and ended in September 1945. The clocks were set to be two hours ahead of Greenwich Mean Time (GMT) during the summer months, then they would go back just one hour during the winter. This was so the local farmers would have more daylight hours to grow crops and foodstuffs. They could also work longer in the fields. Also, munition workers from factories could walk home safely in the light rather than have to travel in the dark. Enemy raids were less likely to take place in light hours, also.

Double summertime meant the West Indians could play their favourite game of cricket until eleven o'clock at night. One could even go out as late as nine o'clock in the evening to start a game of cricket and be able to finish it. In the Caribbean, it would become dark as early as six o'clock in the evening. So this seemed marvellous to them.

When my father was posted to Melksham, the locals had only seen and read about black people in books. They hadn't actually had any experience with them. Naturally, they were curious.

The Jamaicans and small island people would venture out to local village dances. Girls nearby had attended and were a bit unsure of the Caribbean people. Of course, there were the weekend dances. My dad visited the dances to socialise, but he was never a dancer. The popular dances at the time were the jive and the jitterbug. The girls were a bit reluctant to dance at first, so the men started dancing among themselves. But that encouraged a few girls to wander onto the dance floor and partner up with someone. More would follow. Then all of a sudden, all the girls would run onto the dance floor, as if to storm the dance floor.

Smile…

Entertainment in the town comprised the cinema, snooker halls and pubs. My father had learned to play snooker during his time spent here.

There was one time at RAF Melksham (in other camps also) that fifteen hundred troops were struck down by an infectious disease called mumps. The camp had only small hospital quarters, so dining halls were converted to accommodate extra beds. Mumps can be very serious, especially in adult men. The disease can become quite complicated concerning men's nether regions. They can swell up and cause pain. The nurses and doctors were women and they had to inspect the men's delicate lower parts on a regular basis. This caused a lot of laughter—and shyness among the young men!

Luckily, there were no fatalities in people suffering from mumps here. But way back at the Filey camp, my father recalled two airmen who passed away from an infectious disease called meningitis.

# Chapter Thirteen

Later, my father and his fellow servicemen were relocated to camps like RAF Lyneham and Brize Norton, for example. At the weekend, the young men and women would head out to London in groups for some weekend entertainment. They would travel by bus or train. The year was early 1945. It was also easy to hitch-hike anywhere. This was wartime. If any man or woman were walking out in uniform, people would be happy and pleased to take them to anywhere they wanted to go. No money ever passed hands. Men and women in uniform were well respected.

Dad and fellow troops stayed in youth hostels. In fact, on arrival, in London, they would find a hostel near to a dance hall, snooker place and cinema! The boys and girls were going to have fun!

The Paramount Dance Hall was open on a Saturday and Sunday afternoon from 3pm till 6pm, then from 7pm till 11pm. After eleven o'clock, they would all rush over to the Lyceum Ballroom, which was open till four o'clock in the morning. Big band music was popular at this time. The youngsters let their hair down and tried to forget about the war. My dad enjoyed the lively atmosphere and the music was good.

The 77 Club on Wimpole Street would be another place to visit. Also, in West London they would frequent the Hammersmith Palais. The famous band playing at the time would be Joe Loss and His Orchestra. There were trips to

Lyons, the famous coffee and tea house. Middleweight boxing matches were very frequent. My dad enjoyed the boxing matches, especially fighters like the Jamaican Rennie Davis, who would give a good fight. RAF boxers like Jackson Bill, Johnny Carrington and Percy Lewis were well sought-after.

Cinemas like the Gaumont, Movietone and Pathé News were well visited. Film stars like Bing Crosby were discovered and launched into the movies. James Stewart, Humphrey Bogart, Cary Grant, Henry Fonda, Peter Lorre and Kirk Douglas were becoming great movie stars. It was an era when Hollywood became the original town for creating highly paid movie stars. Actors like Hedy Lamarr, Ava Gardner, Rita Haywood, Lana Turner and Ingrid Bergman were made into great movie icons. Cinemas provided a place to visit when there was bad weather or when the troops had a lot of time on their hands.

My father recalls a story where there was a real man playing the organ in the cinema. The troops would be reeling with laughter when he played with such enthusiasm; his arms were waving up into the air, his legs would kick out at the side, so funny was his exaggerated performance!

Another popular place to visit was the Nuffield Centre situated in Wardour Street. It was a huge building donated to the services by Lord Nuffield (William Morris). It was like the London Palladium as we know it in the way there was a variety of entertainment. The shows would last all day long. Servicemen from all over England would arrange to meet there because most people knew how to get there and knew where it was. Long-lost friends were found.

My father was in London during the end of the war. London was on red alert and they endured frequent bombings. In between having fun with friends there were regular bombings in the daytime and at night-time. On hearing the air raid sirens, people had to dive for cover in basements and air raid shelters. So with seeing buildings falling down around you, it was a bit of escapism to go back to the cinema to continue to watch a film. London was severely bombed during the war, the East End particularly. Iconic buildings in the City of Westminster and St Marylebone were badly damaged. And so was Buckingham Palace. My father never spoke about the bombing; he just recalled the good times and the places they all visited...

# Chapter Fourteen

At one minute past twelve on Tuesday 8 May 1945, Churchill announced war was over. This was celebrated as VE Day (Victory in Europe Day). Dad commented about this. He was in Hyde Park. The atmosphere was one of great joy. People were kissing each other, drinking beer and dancing. It was a euphoric feeling...

My father and all servicemen and women returned to their camp. The first year after the end of the war they were very busy. They were always travelling on the road. Materials from the war had to be taken all around the UK and stored. Surplus bombs and ammunition had to be kept safely in various places. The assignment of bombs and weapons were dangerous to move. Huge, long transporters were summoned to take the stuff away, mainly by road, with great care. My father thoroughly enjoyed the reorganisation, for there was plenty of work to be done, but this period came to an end after about a year to eighteen months.

After the sorting out, the RAF Jamaicans were confined to camp. My father talked about his time during this stage, being stationed in the Bristol area. I am not sure whether he stayed at RAF Melksham or whether it was somewhere else; at this stage it is unclear. Anyway, there was very little work to do. The men and women were 'scratching about' trying to find tasks to occupy their day. They all seemed to be washing cars or trucks and polishing them to a very high shine. The walls of buildings needed to be painted. The men called it 'bull'. People pretended to look busy and life became one long bore...

Now, there were various discussions and meetings about whether the young Caribbean people wanted to return to their islands or stay to settle in England. Some people were homesick. They missed their families and friends. My dad wrote letters regularly to family; he loved life in England. There was very little in the way of employment back home in Jamaica. He would live a simple life if he ventured back home, with not much prospect for the future. That is, food was homegrown around his house. Dinner would be caught by fishing in the sea. Life seemed better in England. He said there were more opportunities in England. He could perhaps go to study another trade in the hope of gaining professional employment.

There was a bit of a quandary in the Colonial Office. How were they going to send home over five thousand Jamaicans and island people? Also, it was not just small island people; there were Indians, Africans, Polish, Canadians and people from New Zealand. People had volunteered to help in the war from all over the British Empire.

There was a shortage of ships to take them all home. The regulations were, also, that they had to be accompanied by British officers. Eventually, those who wished to return to their homeland, were drafted to different camps for onward transportation to their home countries.

The British Colonial Office needed to assign a person to deal with all of these issues. A welfare officer was appointed. He was delegated to organise the Colonial Office Rehabilitation Course. He would liaise with the Colonial Office and all persons concerned. There needed to be a lot of sorting out. It was going to be a long process.

Because most of the Caribbean people were perplexed about what to do for the best, they were given two months' leave. This was called 'demob' leave. There were various meetings for them to attend, giving advice. Some attended short-term courses like carpentry or accounting.

After demob leave, the servicemen and women had come to a decision. My father—and many others—decided to sign up to stay in the RAF in England for a further three years. This would give him more time to settle into the British way of life. The three years provided him with food and lodgings and time to plan the future. He didn't want to venture out into civvy (civilian) street too soon, as he was naive about exactly what was out there. After all, this was a new country for him to acclimatise to.

# Chapter Fifteen

Some more fortunate West Indians were enrolled onto courses like accountancy or engineering. My dad's friend went to Leicester Technical College to learn how to make boots and shoes. Others requested the type of training they wanted but were turned down. The choices of training courses were limited. Training was sometimes forced upon them. This created a lot of dissatisfaction among the men and women.

The English people's attitude towards them had now changed. The war was over and all the welcoming and friendliness wasn't there anymore. Among the barracks of the RAF camps they had only themselves to interact with. While being in the military, there must have been some white officers who didn't really like the black island people. But whatever they thought of you was under restrain because of the discipline. After all, there were King's rules and Air Council Instructions. The white officers kept their prejudices concealed and everyone was treated the same.

Going out into civvy street and job interviews was very different in the way of people's acceptance of them. Remember, they also had to find housing. The darker the skin tone, the more the white people turned them away. They would be more accepting of a lighter skinned person than a darker. There was prejudice.

I am going to tell you a couple of stories about the experiences of my father's friends who had left the RAF to search for work and find employment. The prospects in Nottingham seemed good. A Jamaican I shall call Mac went to the local employment exchange.

He remembers his experience as follows: 'On looking for work at the labour exchange and asking, I was told they were keeping their jobs for their "own Englishmen".' Mac had difficulty finding a job he liked, so he just took anything in the hope of finding the job he wanted at a later date.

Alphonse describes how he would go walking the streets, visiting factories and local businesses in the hope of finding work. He told how he would go out all day. He would only get to see the supervisor and not the manager. The receptionists fobbed him off, saying, 'There is no work here.' People were abrupt with him and standoffish. He walked the streets for weeks, choosing different areas, catching a long succession of buses. Each day, he felt a sense of foreboding and was almost in fear of going out because of having to deal with constant rebuffs. The white men would often say, 'Sorry, we don't employ blacks here.'

Alphonse began to feel anger. He had very little choice but to carry on. No way would he give up and lose hope of finding a job.

Many good Jamaicans, small island workers, had their confidence and self-worth eroded. Many never secured the jobs they were trained for or qualified to do. They just had to accept humble pie and go with the flow.

These stories sound unbelievable to me now in the year 2024. Black people suffered great humiliation in those days. They were repeatedly racially abused in the street and most places they visited, but what could they do? They just had to ignore the snide remarks.

One example of a white person asking stupid questions is, 'How do you know when you want to wash?'

When a black worker was recommended for a promotion—which was rare—another worker would say, 'Do you think I want a black man in charge of me?'

Intelligent Jamaicans were often given subservient jobs, even though they proved to be better workers than their white colleagues. They were often asked to sweep the floor and were given dirty jobs to do. It was pure racism.

There was very little in the way of social security benefits. The unemployment benefit wasn't much money. Also, people were too proud to accept money they hadn't worked for, so they wouldn't claim. Unemployment benefits were originally created to be a source of income when someone had found themselves temporarily out of work. The benefit was to be used for bus fares to attend interviews.

On the other hand, a few West Indians had actually found the jobs they had wanted. My dad's friend Mr Petgrave travelled to Scotland to the School of Chiropody. He was recommended by the head of the school for a job in Nottingham, in June 1949, to work in the general dispensary. He had an interview, got the job and stayed for a long time. He then applied for and got the post of sector chiropodist for the City of Nottingham, to develop centres within the health service. He stayed there for six years, then started his own successful practice. Another acquaintance trained to be a school teacher. In the early 60s, she qualified and her career lasted for years, ending up a head teacher.

# Chapter Sixteen

Although the ex-servicemen were facing racial tensions out on civvy street, my father was protected. He had signed on to stay in the RAF for a further three years.

In January 1947, he was stationed at RAF Watnall in Nottinghamshire. There were regular outings with friends when he wasn't working. A gang of servicemen would regularly hop on a train to Nottingham, Leicester, Derby or even Lincolnshire, to be where the action was—mainly to dances. At this time, I know my dad had started to date a girl called Joyce, who lived in Leicester. I really do not know how long the relationship lasted, but he often spoke about her throughout his life. Apparently, she told him she had a disease of the heart. One day, he received a letter through the post to say Joyce had died. She had died of rheumatic heart disease. This memory stayed with him all of his life. And it must have been with great sadness he had to carry on his everyday life without her. Still, the months passed by...

Travelling into Nottingham city centre one evening, they all went to the Palais de Danse. This was an iconic dance hall, which became famous for its afternoon tea dances during and after the war. The Palais de Danse was built in 1925. In this dance hall there was a group of giggling girlfriends and one of them was my mother. She was an English white woman. When my mother and her girlfriends asked my father's name, he replied, 'Just call me Tony.' I suppose with his real name being Emmett Samuel Joseph, it was a bit of an unusual name for people to grasp at the time. My father was then known as 'Tony' for the rest of his life. I will tell you this story in greater detail.

My father met my mother, who was 18 years old. Her name was June. June was at the Palais with her sister, Marie, and some friends. They had become fascinated by the handsome servicemen all dressed up in uniform. Many white girls married Jamaican and small island servicemen. In fact, about half a dozen of the men in Dad's friendship group married English girls.

My mother and father were married in a registry office in Nottingham on the seventh of February 1948. It was a short service. Mum wore a two-piece suit, referred to as a 'costume' in those days. Dad looked handsome wearing his RAF uniform. There were family and friends at the wedding. The reception was held in the local pub.

My mother had lived with her grandmother, Grandma Loach, in Bentinck Street. My father's recollection of Grandma Loach was that she was a very jolly sort of person, a lively, jovial lady who was well known in the neighbourhood for telling the future. She was Scottish and had a broad Scottish accent.

She had told family and friends that she was known as Lady Sarah Jane Bowers in Scotland. She had run away with the chauffeur, Mr Loach, and her own family had now disowned her. They initially travelled to a place called Farnsfield in Nottingham—it might have been with his type of work. Then later, they separated, and she was left on her own with children. I have researched this part of family history and have not found anything to substantiate this story. It could have just been her fantasy...

Anyway, many people would frequent her parlour for palm and tea leaf readings. It was there she would perform her consultations.

The coal fire would burn brightly. A cup of tea would be offered to the person. Friendly banter and chat would take place while 'picking up the vibes'. The person would finish drinking the cup of tea, whereupon she would ask them to turn over their tea cup. Then, a reading of the tea leaves would begin to take place. Grandma Loach added a bit of drama into the mix. She would throw sugar into the fire. A loud 'whoosh' of flames would leap high, brightening the room. This frightened my mother when she was a very young girl, who stood around watching.

My father had got on very well with Grandma Loach and she was fond of him. Dad continued to be based at RAF Watnall but spent a lot of his time with my mother at her grandma's house. Therefore, there were a lot of train journeys to and from RAF Watnall to Nottingham.

# Chapter Seventeen

So after serving his three more years, on 24 January 1950, my father finally left the RAF.

Nottingham was an industrial city with an abundance of job opportunities. A recruitment drive was taking place at the Clifton Colliery. My father secured a job at the coal mine. So did over a hundred ex-servicemen. The type of work involved was strenuous. Men worked on machines and dug out the coalface with pickaxes and shovels. It was indeed a dangerous and dirty job. The wages were excellent though to compensate for this. Compared with other manual work, the coalface workers were highly paid.

My father was an intelligent man and could have easily been trained in accountancy or suchlike, but there was prejudice around. There was prejudice at interviews and then in certain workplaces. I suppose he didn't want the hassle of it all. He just accepted his destined position in life and that was to work down a coal mine.

Dad worked shifts. It could be a day shift, which would start at five o'clock in the morning and finish about four o'clock in the afternoon. A night shift would start at ten o'clock at night and end at six o'clock the next morning. This was called working days or working nights. The pay was really good, especially when he worked the overtime, which was often.

The miners were high earners and started to be able to buy their own houses. My father had developed ambitions.

His desire was to acquire a home of his own for his wife and now baby son, John, to live in. They had lived with Grandma Loach for about five years and had saved enough money to put a deposit down on a house in the Arnold area of Nottingham.

It was a small terraced house on Furlong Avenue. They moved into the little house of their own, a cosy little two-up two-down house, complete with cellar. Like most young couples, Mum and Dad wanted it to be decked out with modern furniture and all mod cons. They visited furniture shops like the big Co-operative stores situated on Parliament Street. Mum was very particular about the colour scheme in her new home. She, like many girls, had left school at 14 years of age. She then learned a skill as a dressmaker and sewing machinist in manufacturing. Mum worked in a fashion house in the Lace Market, Hockley area. So, she bought reams of fabric and made her own curtains with matching sofa cushions for the new house.

Apparently, they were a very happy couple, always hugging and kissing. My father would sing the Jim Reeves melodies popular at the time. They bought a gramophone. This was a solid piece of furniture, which stood upright on the floor. It had an inbuilt radio with loud speaker and record deck on the top. It was made of solid oak and looked like a cabinet when closed up.

At this stage, my father was homesick for the taste of Caribbean food. So, on a Sunday, he would 'take over' the kitchen, showing my mother how to cook rice and peas with curried chicken, Jamaica's national food. Most Jamaican mothers teach their sons how to cook, so Dad was a good cook.

Mum loved to play the big band records. Bands like Glenn Miller, Tommy Dorsey and Humphrey Lyttelton were popular.

She would often sing and hum songs like 'I Double Dare You', 'The Fish Seller' and also 'The Onions' by Humphrey Lyttelton and his Orchestra. A feeling of happiness and contentment swirled around the home. Mum would often cease her chores when a song she liked came on the radio. She would pick up the hem of her 1950s voluminous skirt and dance around the kitchen. Dad singing, clicking his fingers, Mum, waltzing. Picture the scene...

# Chapter Eighteen

In the 1950s, there was a lot of rebuilding of homes and factories. Britain began manufacturing again. People wanted to work to earn money so they could buy nice things for their homes. Housewives began to buy gadgets. Hoover vacuum cleaners were being made and sold to fulfil the need of the housewife, so she could spend less time performing household chores. Women wanted modern kitchen equipment, such as electric food mixers and washing machines. Before the use of domestic washing machines, housewives would roll their sleeves up. They had to scrub the dirt out of the clothes by hand with soap—usually a large green-coloured block of soap, for soap powders were only just being commercialised.

They would then have to rinse the clothes in clean water. The clothes would then be squeezed through an iron mangle. The mangle consisted of two rollers. They would revolve when the housewife turned the handle. The dripping wet clothes would be pushed through manually and the rollers would squeeze out most of the water. It was indeed a really long laborious chore.

This was the beginning of a new era, an era of optimism. People started to purchase carpets for their houses, as carpets were becoming affordable to the working-class man. My father continued to work very hard and soon, their house was filled with new machinery and gadgets like the vacuum cleaner. I remember the cylindrical vacuum cleaner, when turned on, was a noisy beast in our living room. Mum was house-proud. She kept the front living room 'for best'.

There was a new three-piece suite made of faux crocodile leather. The comfortable sofa and chairs were the colour of dark green, like a crocodile itself...

A red carpet covered the floor and suitable matching curtains adorned the windows. The room was only used when visitors came round. We lived mainly in the dining room and kitchen part of the house.

Motor cars being were manufactured. There were advertisements for the American Ford Motor Company advertising family cars. Now there were very few cars driven on English roads at this time. Only someone like a doctor, or other professionals, would own a car, for it was expensive to buy and to maintain the upkeep of it. It was really looked upon as a luxury item to own.

It was quite rare for an average working-class family to actually own their own motor car, but my father, at this time, as I said, was very hardworking. On his way home from work, he would often stop at the Ford Motor car showrooms. (There was one just off Derby Road in Nottingham called Hooleys.) The motor cars on display were gorgeous. One day, he went home to my mother and told her about the lovely grey-beige and cream-coloured car he had got his 'eye on'. He took my mother to have a look at it...

It was a 187 Ford Zephyr Zodiac (1954), spectacular looking, complete with white wheels. He took a test drive, fell in love with it and bought it. This was his first motor car ever. He had seen photographs of cars in magazines. The time had come when he could actually acquire such a vehicle he had only dreamed of before.

On reflection, my Jamaican father must have been dazzled by the material things he could buy. He became 'carried away' by his buying power. Remember, he came from a family and lifestyle where possession of material things was not necessarily needed to enjoy life. Also, it was probably frowned upon in the church-going communities. When he had been to Kingston in Jamaica to work as a young man, he had seen the riches of the haberdashery shop owner. My father had become materialistic.

Because motor cars were rarely seen, seeing one owned by a working-class family, his neighbours began to make comments. When Dad would drive his family into Arnold for a shopping trip, people would pass comments like, 'You know where he got the money to buy that?' and they would look at my mum as if to suggest that she was a woman of ill repute. After all, she was a white woman with a black man. There were racial expletives thrown in their direction, suggesting Dad was a pimp with his prostitute. This absolutely enraged my father.

The coronation of Queen Elizabeth II took place in June 1953, in London. In the same year, in the winter months when coal fires were lit, a great problem emerged. On cold foggy days, the fog would combine with industrial smoke and smoke from coal fires emanating from people's homes. This was called smog. Vision on the streets was so bad. Buses, lorries and cars were discouraged from venturing out into the roads for fear of accidents.

The smog was smoky and acrid. The air was foul. Hospitals were becoming full of people with breathing difficulties. Four thousand people died in London alone. The Great Smog lasted for four days in London. But the smog became prevalent in many other cities, including Nottingham. People began to wear masks to cover their faces in order to protect themselves. They called these fogs 'pea-soupers' because of their greenish sulphurous appearance. Actual fog would begin to seep into houses, through the window and underneath the outside doors, for it was single-pane glass in those days. Double-glazed windows were not very popular at this time.

In 1956, the Clean Air Act was passed through Parliament. This was to help stop pollution of the air. There was an introduction of smokeless fuel. People at home were steered towards burning smokeless fuel in their fireplaces. But the air didn't become clean overnight. In fact, I remember witnessing pea-souper fogs when I was a child in the early 60s. The fog descended in the winter and it was impossible to see more than two feet in front of you. If the fog came down when in the car on the road, you had to drive so slowly and creep along for fear of crashing into someone or something. I remember it being very frightening at the time.

# Chapter Nineteen

After a few years, the two-up two-down house seemed too small for their growing family. My sister Dawn was born, following her, another son, Christopher, came along, then me.

My mother was a tall, attractive woman. She stood five feet eight inches in her bare feet, with a slim, willowy figure. Her straight chestnut hair was curled into the modern look of the 1940s and 1950s. She would always dress immaculately—as many women did in this era. Her two-piece costume (suit) would be worn, even just popping out to the local grocery store. A cloche-style feathered hat would be placed 'just so' on her head. She wore stockings with a seam running from the top of the leg to the bottom, as was the style at the time. Her shoes were high stiletto heels. Handbag in place, she must have looked the 'bee's knees' walking down that road, pushing her coach-built green and cream Silver Cross pram.

In Arnold in Nottingham, they were building some brand-new detached houses. So our house was sold and we moved to a newbuild on Castleton Avenue. Again, the house was fitted with furnishings and fittings fit for a queen. Mum was even more house-proud with her colour-coordinated sitting room, kept for best, for visitors only. Though I remember my mother saying, 'The house feels cold. Even with the fire blazing, it always has a chill about it.'

Remember, there were only coal fires for heating. The floors in this house were made of solid concrete, not floorboards. Maybe this was the reason the house always felt cold.

My brother Christopher was a lively boy, who was always poorly with terrible colds and bad coughs. Later, he started to suffer the symptoms of asthma. He would cough, wheeze and become out of breath. My father thought it was the cold house which contributed to his illness.

I do remember this house, for I was just a toddler. The steps at the side of it were very steep. I had great difficulty climbing those steps. I clambered onto one and then another until I had found myself inside the kitchen. Again, I could hear the sound of the gramophone playing from further inside. Dad could not dance but would just click his fingers in time to the beat. He would sing to the tunes of Jim Reeves and many other country and western artists. He liked a song that told a story. The house was joyful with sounds of laughter.

Mum and Dad were happy with their now four children. I recall a time when I was three or four years old, it was the days when kids played out in the street. At the top of our road was a cul-de-sac. All of the children would play ball games, hide-and-seek and of course, the go- carts would be trundled up the steep slope, with children screaming with excitement as they whizzed down. The older girls would skip in the street, with skipping ropes. The other kids were accepting of us, the children with the wild hair...

The idea of mixed-raced kids was fairly new at the time. Our white British neighbours didn't like us. Us kids had thick dark frizzy hair, different from my mother's chestnut-coloured hair. We were commonly referred to as 'half-caste'. My mother and father were often called names in the street. They would call my mum a 'prostitute' and asked why she was with that 'blackie'.

In the shops, when together, people would stare and snigger. When my dad walked out on his own, he was called a stupid 'n*****' and such phrases as 'Why don't you go back to your own country?' often followed. The racial abuse was horrendous. In the end, my mother stopped going out with my dad to the shops and preferred to go on her own. On going out, her next-door neighbour would walk towards her, disapprovingly making a face and swiftly crossed the road. My mother was called names like 'n***** lover' and we were called 'black bastards'. It wasn't very nice. When she arrived back home, she would cry. One night, an envelope was pushed through our letterbox. It contained dog shit.

In August 1958, there was an incident in St Ann's, Nottingham. It all began in a pub. A group of Jamaican men were walking into the pub with white women, holding hands and romancing. Laughing and chatting and generally having a good time. Well, the white men objected to the men fraternising with 'their' white women. A few nasty words were exchanged, racially motivated words, so fighting broke out. All being young men and women, on a hot summer's night, the fighting spilled out into the street. As other young people were passing by, they too joined in or got caught up in the scuffle. Well, the police and ambulance were called to sort it out and take away people with minor injuries.

The next day, it was reported, in the news, there had been a 'Race Riot'. In fact, it wasn't such a big deal as the newspapers had reported. My father talked about it later and said it was just a crowd of about twenty people, all races, punching each other. He wasn't involved, being a family man with wife and children, and being at home.

# Chapter Twenty

Jamaica was still part of the great British Empire. Jamaicans spoke very good English in this era. Their accents were of high-class English gentlemen. They thought they had to speak this way, after coming to England. Jamaican women spoke impeccable English, often using 'big' words in their conversations. The working-class white English folk must have thought it was hilarious, because they, themselves, didn't speak like that. In fact, sometimes white folks would remark at their 'posh' accents or even 'titter' at the Jamaican people. But this was the way it was, at the time. Black people were referred to as being 'coloured'. This was a polite and well-mannered word to use. Like when describing a black man in a shop, you used the word 'coloured' and not black. My father referred to himself as being a coloured man and accepted this terminology.

Like many Caribbean young men and women, they were brought up mostly by strict parents. They were chastised often. Everybody knew each other in the parishes back home. Folk would gossip about you if they'd seen any wrongdoing. So children had to be good by attending their churches on Sunday. They were taught right from wrong. The Ten Commandments always came into play in their everyday lives. They were God-fearing, proud people.

I haven't yet described my father at this stage in his life. Dad was very well spoken. He chose his words carefully. In a conversation, especially to a stranger, he would throw in a long word or phrase, like 'extremities' or 'appertaining to'.

He would say to the family, 'Your body is your temple, so treat it respectfully.' My father had a very kind, smiley pretty-boy face, with a smart moustache trimmed perfectly above his top lip. He was mostly an optimistic kind of a guy. Always outwardly upbeat and wise with his words. When he spoke, he was very positive and excitable, often bringing laughter into whatever he had to say.

He would always be well turned out. A shirt and tie would always be worn when going out of the house to do some shopping, or whatever. People, in this time, did dress smartly, because the social class system was so pronounced and set in stone. He always wore a hat, for example, to finish off his outfit. People would judge you for the way you looked. So, to be accepted, he would dress very smartly. I can still picture him now polishing his shoes, to a very high standard. Wherever he went, he would suddenly turn on his heel and walk off at great speed. His pace was always quick and his steps precise.

My Jamaican father was not very tall in height. In his socks he stood five feet seven. I knew he would have liked to have been taller because whenever he stopped in the street to speak to someone, he would lift himself up by rocking to and fro on the balls of his feet, pushing himself up, thus making him appear a little taller. Later in life, he actually inserted wooden blocks, specially made, into the back of his shoes, to elevate him slightly.

My father was not great at interpersonal relationships. There seemed to be a distance in the way he would connect with you. I always felt that he was putting on a show and that the real 'him' was somewhat buried. He was not an outwardly affectionate person to his children. Although he would often smile, which shows he did care.

Anyway, back to the story. The house in Castleton Avenue was sold. It was February 1961. I do clearly remember the day we actually moved. The house was packed up. A huge removal van came and the men loaded up the boxes.

I can remember my mother walking from the house with her coach-built Silver Cross pram. She had decided to walk to the new place. It wasn't too far away. I was walking at her side, holding onto the pram. I clearly remember the scene, a snapshot in my mind. The picture I can recall at any time. My brother John was a lot older than me and Christopher was five years old. John hitched a lift with the removal men, probably to show them the way to the new home. Christopher and Dawn travelled in the car with my father. The walk took us about twenty minutes. We soon arrived at our new home in Woodthorpe.

It was wintertime. With the winter came the frosts and the snow. It was not snowing on our removal day, but it was cold and damp. The memories of walking into our newly built home came with the smell of new timber. The scent of sawdust and new wood. The house had a fireplace in the lounge. The first task my dad performed was to light a fire in the hearth. This was the only form of heating. Central heating was only just becoming affordable and being installed in homes.

The road outside was unmade. It was just a dirt track made up of compressed mud trampled down by the lorries and tractors moving up and down, bringing sand and bricks for the developing building site. We lived at the top of Nordean Road.

The house had a very big garden, all unmade. Just a pile of soil with stones and rubble mixed in. At the boundary, at the top of the garden, were two large hawthorn trees. At the back of the boundary were fields. It was all fields, stretching back as far as Arnold Lane. Just in the back of our garden, in a field outside of the boundary, stood a large oak tree.

My brother John had always loved the outdoors. This usually involved climbing trees. So, straight away, he started the building of a tree house in the middle of the huge oak tree's spreading branches. There was an abundance of material to use, for the building site was full of pieces of wood, all stacked up outside the half-built houses.

John was good with his hands. He quickly made a stepladder, rickety though. Bits of nails and twine would hold the creation together. He placed it upright against the oak tree, then climbed. When at the top of the ladder, he cut a few branches so he could lay a large sheet of plywood across a few lengths of branch to make a flat surface. He held it in place by knocking a few nails into the plywood and then into the tree. He then found a piece of tarpaulin from our father's garage and tied it into place with pieces of rope.

We all climbed up the ladder and into our little tree house. I say 'all', but it was just John, Chris and Dawn. John had to lift me up into it because I was only four years old. I remember only going inside the one time.

Meanwhile, my father was working hard at the Gedling Colliery. His shift work took over the weekends. He could earn another half a week's wages, just in a weekend. He must have been very tired, especially when he had to plan the layout of a brand-new garden.

My father was a natural gardener. He would wear a dark-blue boiler suit to protect his clothes, then spend all day in the garden. He knew how to prepare a new lawn. I can still see him now, holding his spade, turning over the soil. Dad would then rest on his spade to smoke a cigarette. He would smoke about ten cigarettes a day. It was very stylish to smoke in those days. One would look like a film star.

My father's new garden was truly landscaped. He would measure out the boundaries of the lawn, then measure a border where the flower beds would be. He set the boundaries by using string and garden twine. He even measured out a vegetable patch (a large plot), which was situated towards the back of the garden. A load of farmyard manure would be ordered and stealthily dug into the vegetable plot.

Dad had ordered privet hedging plants to be delivered. When delivered, he would carefully space the plants out and then plant them, to make the boundary hedge.

# Chapter Twenty-One

After the upheaval of moving house, we all settled down to family life on Walsingham Road. The weeks passed by. Mum and Dad were busy. Mum looking after all of her children and baby Sharon, who was only a few months old. Dad busy working all the hours God sent and otherwise outside in his beloved garden. John and Dawn had gone back to school. Christopher, as I have already explained, was always ill with bad coughs and colds. This had developed into asthma. He was being treated at the local Children's Hospital, situated just off the Mansfield Road. My mother and father regularly visited the outpatients department with Christopher. Also, he was regularly an inpatient. Always in and out of hospital, with bronchial problems.

Christopher had been given a three-wheeler bike for his birthday. It was a Pashley-type bike, which was fashionable at the time. Christopher was at the helm while I often rode pillion on the back. There was a metal blue box, like a trunk, attached to the rear. It was like the old-fashioned bread bins, where when the lid was lifted, it rolled back inside the top. I would lift the lid and actually climb into the box, whereupon Chris would peddle off fast, me holding on for dear life! When he rode on his own, the metal box at the back would rattle. He loved to ride the bike up and down the back path. The trike was his pride and joy.

I have to tell you about what happened next, the saddest day of my father's life…

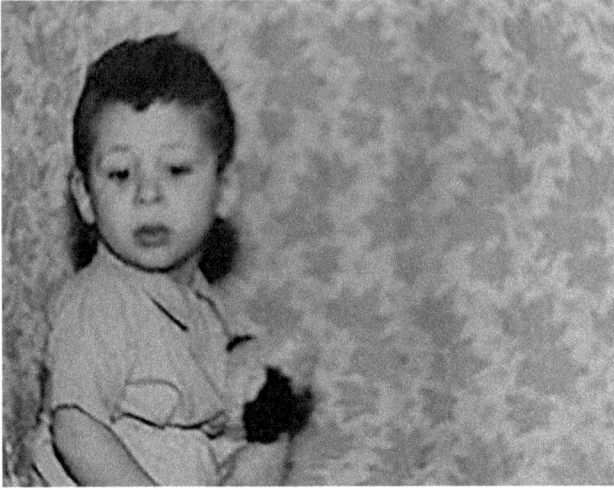

It was the twenty-ninth of April 1961. The day his dearly beloved son Christopher died. He was five years old. I can recall this traumatic day, for it stays crystal-clear in my mind, like a series of snapshots, a sequence of events.

Firstly, it was in the morning, a Saturday morning. My mother was standing just outside the back door, talking to the neighbour. A small wire fence attached to two concrete posts separated them. Christopher was poorly, suffering with an asthma attack. He was wearing his pyjamas, lying on the settee, covered by a blanket. As I stood by him, he gasped, 'Get Mommy, get Mommy.' I ran to Mum outside. She was wearing a 50s-style, white cotton skirt, patterned with an array of large bright orange flowers scattered all over it. I remember it well.

I started muttering, 'Mommy, Chrit-e-pah...' for I couldn't yet pronounce his name. She said something like, 'Wait, I'm talking.' I ran back inside into the living room to tell Christopher. He was, by now, gasping for breath. I could see a trickle of dark brown blood coming from his nose. It wasn't the bright red blood that comes from your knee when you fall over and hurt yourself. The blood was dark. I ran back to Mum, who was still talking outside. I tugged frantically at her skirt and blurted out, 'Mommy, Chrit-e-pah blood!' Straight away, she dashed inside the house. Then all panic, bedlam, confusion, heartache happened.

The snapshot in my mind, as I recall, was my father suddenly appeared in the living room. He was wearing a pair of striped pyjamas. Dad must have been working nights at the pit so had to sleep upstairs in the daytime and was woken up by my mum. My father picked Christopher up from the settee and placed him onto the carpeted floor. I then remember the appearance of my brother John and sister Dawn. My father had asked John to run down the road to the telephone box to call an ambulance.

Very quickly, two ambulance men walked into our living room. My father was giving mouth-to-mouth resuscitation to Christopher. Then, the ambulance men took over. Meanwhile, I was standing there watching all of this unfold. I looked over at my father to see the tears rolling down his face. I knew, in my four-year-old mind, that something absolutely dreadful and awful had happened. My memory was that I was in complete and utter turmoil. The ambulance men suggested we children should be taken outside. We were all crying: John, Dawn and me. We went into 'automatic' mode and, strangely, we all stood in a line, side by side, in the back garden.

My brother and sister did not utter a word. They just stood silently, crying. I took my place at Dawn's side and waited. Then after a while, I started to run around like a deranged person, crying, then screaming. Yet nobody spoke. Nobody explained what was happening. I looked up at John and Dawn and they were still silent and tearful. The snapshot now ends.

I can no longer tell you any more detail about what happened next. My mind goes blank. I still feel traumatised writing this now. My tears are slowly falling onto this page. The image of my father, tears rolling down his grief-stricken face, holding his little child, still haunts me to this day.

I was the only sibling to recall all of the events on this awful tragic day. Sharon, my other sister, was safely tucked up in her cot, fast asleep. Unaware. Safe in slumber.

My brother John and sister Dawn will have their own version of events. Indeed, in later years, we all talked about what had actually happened. John was about 13 years old.

John had told me that Dad did not want Christopher to be taken away straight away. Instead, my father carried him upstairs and laid him out on his bed. There, he stayed the same evening and throughout the night. It was said, we all knelt and prayed at his bedside.

A flash of memory comes back, I do remember the cream-coloured wrought-iron single bed. But I do not have any images of Christopher lying there, nor can I envisage his mortal face. The next day, he was taken away to what I believe to be the funeral parlour. My mother later recalled, 'They came with a zip-up black bag, put him in it, zipped him up and took him away.' I cannot remember this. All I remember is going to the funeral director's with my father.

This was at Baguley's funeral parlour on Mansfield Road. Walking through to a lounge area, there were two awkward triangular-shaped steps which took you down to a lower area. I distinctively recall looking down and trying to be careful not to fall on those two steps. It's strange, isn't it, what snippets of information stay in the mind at times of trauma. I suppose some snippets the mind chooses to forget, also.

The day of the funeral came. John and Dawn went to school, as usual. I was taken to the service, which was held in a small chapel at Redhill Cemetery. A hymn was sung, one of many. The words, 'Yea, though I walk in the valley of the shadow of death, I will fear no evil'—Psalm 23:4, otherwise known as 'The Lord Is My Shepherd'. The poignant words stuck in my mind. Even when I hear those words now, I stop to listen and my mind goes back to the day I first heard them, at Christopher's funeral.

Christopher's death was never explained to me. The subject, in the family, was hardly discussed. There seemed to be an awkwardness in the air. Family members being abrupt with each other and then arguments breaking out. I suppose, in 1961, some things were never talked about. Talking was not in vogue. 'Just sweep it under the carpet and it will go away and everything will be alright...'

My father had always had a short temper and had no time for fools. This became more apparent, together with a developing anger. My Jamaican father continued to work all the hours of the day down that dark and dirty coal mine. We hardly saw much of him.

The weeks flew by. Mum was busy looking after her four children, which included one baby. I remember my mother would set the knives and forks onto the table, counting the usual number of place settings. This time, she would suddenly realise, there was one less. Tears would gush from her eyes. For her, the reality was that Christopher was never going to sit at our dinner table, ever again.

Mum was alone in the house most days, starved of adult company, except for Dad. My father would often work in the evening, or all night long. I can recall, many times, after going to bed, I would get up to walk down the stairs to see my mother sitting alone in the living room. She would be listening to Radio 4 on the old radiogram. I went to her for a cuddle, but she was unable to comfort me and promptly marched me off to bed. She wanted to be alone. When I got back into bed, I cried.

I remember the tune 'Sailing By'. It was often played by an orchestra, on the radio. The music was written by a man called Ronald Binge. Even now, every time I hear the song, it sends me back to that lonely time and I picture my heartbroken mother, sitting alone, having just lost her little boy.

# Chapter Twenty-Two

In our house, money was tight. Indeed, in those days, most working-class people had very little spare cash to spend after all of the bills had been paid out each week. There was no such thing as credit cards. Or little in the way of bank loans either. If you had no money in your purse, that was it: you literally had no money to spend until the next week's pay day. Most people were paid their wages in cash on a Friday at the end of each week. Folk like teachers and doctors were paid monthly into their bank accounts.

The new house was proving to be expensive. When you live in one of the best addresses in Nottingham, the rateable value of a property is high. Have you ever heard of 'bread and butter' houses? It means all of the money is spent on a high mortgage and maintaining a house. There is very little left to spend on food, so you exist on eating bread and butter. That was us. We lived in a lovely detached house in a nice neighbourhood, but we were cash poor. However, I suspect there were a lot of families like us, keeping up appearances.

I can recall being at junior school. On a Monday morning, the teacher collected the dinner money. It cost five shillings per week to have a midday dinner at school every day. In those days, five shillings were two half crowns (coins). I remember asking my mother for the dinner money. She replied, saying she had no money to give me. So, I went to school. All of the girls and boys who wanted to have school dinners stood in a line at the teacher's desk with their dinner money. Well, I also stood in the line. When it was my turn to hand my money over, I had to make an excuse that I'd lost it on the way to school. I felt my face glowing bright red. I felt a great sense of humiliation. The teacher said, 'Bring it tomorrow.' Well, tomorrow came and I still didn't have any money to give. This would sometimes go on for a number of weeks.

My mother would walk down to a shop called Marsden, on Thackeray's Lane. It was always on a Friday. Mum would walk with her Silver Cross pram and her children would skip or run by her side. She was going to shop for her weekly groceries. They sold their digestive biscuits by the pound, in weight. They were bagged up into a greaseproof paper bag.

The English Cheddar cheese appeared as a huge block of cheese which was kept in a counter fridge. My mother would ask for a pound of cheese. The grocer would place the huge block of cheese onto a cold marble slab. With a thin wire attached to the slab, he would slice a piece of cheese off, then put it on the weighing scales. Thereupon, it would be wrapped up neatly in greaseproof paper. The actual price would then be scribbled, in pencil, on the top.

In those days, my mother would just have basic groceries: flour, butter, eggs, meat, vegetables and fruit. Mum was a housewife and she would make her own cakes, pies and dinners. There was no such thing as snack foods, except for packets of crisps. She would make her own stews with suet dumplings cooked in a pressure cooker. Cheap cuts of meat would be bought, like 'scrag end of mutton'. These tough cuts of meat would be cooked under high pressure, therefore making them a bit more tender to eat. My mother's weekly groceries, bought at this shop, would always cost five pounds in money. The groceries would be boxed up and a boy would deliver them to our house on a pushbike, at no extra cost.

The winter of 1962–1963 was really cold and snowy. It was an especially bad winter, according to British records. I remember looking out of the back bedroom window. The snow lay thick on the ground. I watched the sky while huge flakes of fluffy snow floated gently to the ground. All through the night, layer by layer, the snow continued to fall. When I woke up in the morning, the snow lay deep, about one foot, as in twelve inches, deep. We all tried to open the front door, but couldn't.

The snow had drifted up the door, as if to barricade us in. We couldn't open it. We pushed against it, but the heavy weight of the snow made it difficult. My sister decided the best way to deal with the situation was to take a coal shovel from the hearth, walk out of the sheltered back door and go down the side path to the front door. There, she could shovel the snow away. She scraped the snow off the door and threw it to one side, creating a huge lumpy pile. We tried the door again and this time it opened. We had wanted to clear the snow for our mother and father, and enjoyed the challenge.

It was a school day. Wearing our Wellington boots, we wandered through the thick snow down the road to our school. Yes, all schools were expected to be open all of term time. The way of communication in the 60s was by word of mouth, or by telephone, which we didn't have in our house at the time. School staff lived close to the school, so they could walk to work when there was inclement weather. There were no mobile phone text messages or computer email systems! The school would always be open, no matter what the weather was like.

The roads were silent. Cars were firmly stuck in their driveways. A kind of stillness took over, as if the world had ended. Blankets of snow insulated the houses, covering the roof tops.

At about four o'clock in the afternoon, we sisters had walked home from school. We took off our hats and coats inside the house. Peering out of the front window, I noticed a figure walking up our driveway. It had continued to snow all day. The figure wore a cap on its head. I looked further to see a 'growth' of snow on top of the cap. I could now see it was my father!

I ran to open the door and all us sisters laughed. He wore a heavy overcoat and the flat cap was perched on his head. The snow had settled on the top of his cap, layer upon layer. I can still see a picture of my father and all the snow piled up on the top of his cap. It was really funny. At least a four-inch stack of snow had fallen on top of his head. Such a comical site to be seen. Even Dad had looked into the mirror and laughed!

The snow had lasted for weeks on end. The BBC news channel had called it the Big Freeze of 1963. In the north of Yorkshire, roads were impassable. There were snowdrifts ten feet high. Most villages were completely cut off. The night frosts were severe, with plummeting temperatures down to -17°C. Apparently, the snow had started to fall on the Boxing Day of Christmas 1962 and continued to fall until the March of 1963. It was extremely cold weather, and the north-east wind blowing made it feel even colder.

The snow ploughs ventured onto country roads to try to clear them so the local village people could be freed. But it became an impossible task, as more snow fell and the wind made it drift. The ploughs became stuck in ten-foot-high snowdrifts. The East Midlands became paralysed, with many roads blocked with packed ice and piles of snow. The airport was closed for a long spell. As a result, food was running out in local shops.

My father made memorable fires, which he built in the hearth at home. He would build a fire using coal. They were memorable for the way in which he stacked the coal up high into the back of the fireplace. When the fire was all aglow, the heat given off was extremely and breathtakingly hot! Remember, there was only one room in the whole house that contained a fireplace. When Dad made such huge fires, sometimes hot coals would break off and tumble down, past the tiled hearth and onto the rug. Someone would have to be quick to pick up the dustpan and scoop up the rogue piece of burning coal and flick it back into the fire.

The fireplace really should not have been left unattended because of the chance that falling pieces of burning coal could have set fire to the rug. We eventually had a fire guard fitted. This was a metal oval-shaped piece of meshed wire, which stood up on its own. It was placed in front of the coal fire. In the eventuality of a rogue coal falling, it would be contained on the tiles of the hearth.

In the morning, I would wake up and get up out of my bed to look out of the window. Wrapping a blanket around me, I would be shivering. The glass pane would be iced up on the inside. There would be intricate lacy patterns of ice sculptured onto the glass. I would scrape my finger on the ice to create a small hole, where I could peep through the window to find out what the weather was like outside. I would then dash back into bed, taking my school uniform with me, where I would warm it up with my body heat before putting it on. I did this every morning in wintertime. It was a way of life. House central heating systems with radiators were just becoming affordable to the everyday working-class man.

Sometimes, the snow would drift up to six feet high in some places—especially when people cleared the snow from their paths and driveways; the snow would be stacked up really high. Mountains of snow would remain there for weeks, sometimes months, slowly thawing when the spring sunshine began to warm the ground.

In later winters, I remember once we built an actual igloo. My sisters and I prepared brick-like shapes of packed snow. Then we would start to build. The snow house was alright until we attempted to put on the roof. We tried to mould the snow into a roof-like covering. It stayed together for about ten minutes while we sat inside our igloo. Then suddenly, it all collapsed all over us. What fun!

One day, we had built two huge five-foot snowmen on the back lawn. Us sisters were very proud of them. Our brother, John, had walked down the path and he saw them. He gathered up the snow to make snowballs, then pelted our snowmen, destroying their heads. He just laughed and walked off into the house.

# Chapter Twenty-Three

My Jamaican father took to studying the race horses. This meant he would buy a newspaper, usually *Sporting Life*. He would read all about a certain horse that he favoured to win a race. He would be quite intelligent about it. Each horse had its own history, especially regarding the races it had previously won. The age of the horse came into consideration. The weather conditions also were taken into account. Whether the ground was going to be hard or soft. Whether the horse won its last race on soft turf or hard. What was the weather going to be like on the day. He never actually visited a live racecourse meeting though, which probably would have been a little more exciting.

Dad's wages were paid in cash, on a Friday. The money, in bank notes, was given to him inside a little brown envelope. Now, I remember one particular incident. He would always give my mother some housekeeping money. Religiously, he would leave the cash on the mantelpiece, secured by a vase plonked on the top. On this particular Friday, there was no money left there in the usual place. Apparently, Dad had gambled away all of his wages. Indeed, he had put all of his money on a horse that never won. This was terrible. As you can imagine, my mother and father had an almighty argument.

My father had studied the form of a horse and in his mind, it was sure to win the race. He must have been so certain the horse would win. As a result, we had nothing to buy food for the week. The cupboard was certainly very bare.

My father must have quickly realised his stupidity and he never ever repeated his actions with so much money. At the time, he had heard of fellow coal miners winning lots of money by gambling on the horses. So, he must have been egged on by what he had heard. Or maybe it was a moment of madness that had manifested itself as a reaction to Christopher dying. Perhaps a form of release from bereavement. After all, gambling or repeated gambling can sometimes be due to low mood, so they say. Possibly, the thought of winning can lift the spirits. While the race is being won, the feeling of euphoria can take hold. A sudden rush of great joy perhaps.

My father had learned his lesson and changed his ways. Now, he would have a bit of fun with the horses, but this time, by sitting in his armchair at home—not at the bookies.

So later, every Saturday, Dad would buy a copy of the *Sporting Life* newspaper. He would study the horses and their form. Then he would choose a horse to win but would not visit the betting shop to place a bet. He would just switch the television on and sit in the comfort of his armchair and enjoy watching the race. My father had become more tame and really enjoyed the sport.

At this juncture, reader, may I just mention, at this time, Jamaicans, small island people, were a very close-knit community in Nottingham. They would often meet up in each other's houses to host 'blues parties'. Their own music was played, often Jamaican ska. Recordings by popular ska, bluebeat and calypso bands were blasted out. The women cooked their curries, with rice and peas, for some people were homesick. These gatherings made them feel more at home.

There was a savings scheme plan organised by local West Indians. The scheme was for twenty or so people, who would put a pound into a kitty. So in total, there would be twenty pounds in the pot. They took it in turns for someone to take all of the money. This was done regularly so that everybody had their fair share. This scheme could help people to buy furniture, have a holiday or simply help pay for rent.

My father had a fondness for large Ford automobiles. Dad had bought a car, a Ford Zephyr Zodiac. The colour was green and cream, with white wheels. Dad absolutely worshipped it.

Every Sunday, he would fill a bucket of water and wash his beloved car. When it was dry, he would rub in copious amounts of cream-coloured car polish. He would then buff it up until it literally glistened and gleamed in the bright sunlight. He rubbed and rubbed until it reached showroom standard. The seats inside were long bench seats. The huge steering wheel housed a column gear change. I remember he often struggled with the gear change system at first, but soon got the hang of it, for he had learned to drive heavy trucks in the RAF, not actual cars!

Whenever he nipped out to the shops, or wherever, he would ask us girls whether we wanted to go with him for the ride. All of us could fit along the enormous bench seat in the front of the car. Picture the scene, all us daughters huddled up together, and Dad at the wheel. (If you are wondering where our John was at this time, being a lot older than us, he was doing his own thing.)

There were no seat belts to clip on either, as there was no seat belt law in the 60s. He would visit a local scrapyard. There, he would root around for, maybe, a spare part for his engine or a piece of rubber hose. When his radiator sprang a leaky hole, he would go off to the scrapyard to try to find a similar replacement radiator for his beloved Zodiac. At the yard, there would be a pile of exhaust systems, a pile of alternators and so on. So, you just had to sift through everything to find what you wanted. It was a very popular place to go for working-class men, and interesting as to what you could find for a giveaway price.

On a Sunday, we would often 'go for a run' in the Zodiac. I suppose you would call it a trip outdoors. Mum, Dad, all of us would take a trip up the Ollerton Road, which led to Sherwood Forest or Clumber Park. My father would really put his foot down on the accelerator. He liked to drive frighteningly fast. It was a straight road with a central lane for overtaking. So I suppose it was safe enough. I remember my mother would shout, 'Slow down, Tony', especially when he overtook other cars. She was terrified. Us girls were scared also and I closed my eyes often and cowered down into the footwell in between the front and back seats.

My father had decided to have a night out without my mother. He went into the city to Yates's public house by the Old Market Square. This was the meeting place for a lot of Jamaicans who were ex-servicemen. They would have a few drinks and talk about the old times. His favourite drink was rum and blackcurrant, locally known as 'rum and black'. Dad loved the Navy rum. Anyway, in those days, you could drink as much as you liked and still get into your car and drive it home. There were no drink and drive laws.

So, I remember waking up late at night, after Christopher had died, to hear my father unlock the front door and stumble up the stairs to bed. The next day, he told my mother that he had had a lot to drink in the pub and then got into the car and driven home. Apparently, the Zodiac had suddenly stopped while he was driving. He couldn't get it started again, so he had pushed it off the main road and into the petrol station on Woodborough Road. The petrol station was closed for the night, so he had abandoned it there and promptly staggered home. The next day, he had walked to fetch the car. He found it had just run out of petrol; that was all that was wrong with it. It could have been the case that the petrol gauge wasn't functioning properly, or whatever...

# Chapter Twenty-Four

A few years passed by. The now four daughters (for my mother gave birth to another baby girl) and one son were growing up nicely. My father still worked hard down the coal mine. His passion in life was gardening. Regularly, he mowed the lawns, front and back. I can picture him now in his dark-blue boiler suit. After he had mowed, he then bent down with a pair of shears to clip the edge of the lawn. My word, the lawns and garden were immaculate. Everything was kept neat and very tidy.

There was a flower bed at the side of the lawn, where my dad grew dahlias. Dad's beloved dahlias. I sigh. He took to growing every different type and variety of dahlia. The large spiky type, the small deeply clustered headed ones. The taller ones, which had to be staked so their soft fleshy stalks would not snap over in the wind. He had a long, large flower bed full of them. They would bloom in the summertime, when he would cut the stems to bring them indoors. He would then place them on a piece of newspaper beside the kitchen sink. My mother would then proceed to cut the stems down to size and place them in various vases. I remember the flower petals were always full of earwig-type creatures!

In the meantime, things were not going well for my dear mother. She started to do strange things. The memory is clear in my mind. My sisters and I were playing outside in the back garden. We had got our buckets and spades out. One of us was filling a bucket with garden soil. Then water was added, which made it turn into a brown sticky liquid of mud. We all played, adding daisies to our buckets, buttercups also. We played very well, making mud pies. Some mud pies would become more solid. It was a warm day.

The neighbour next door had her washing pegged out onto her washing line. I see it clearly in my mind what happened next. My mother appeared at my side. She picked up my bucket and walked to the privet hedge. Beyond the hedge was the neighbour's washing line, complete with all of her husband's shirts. They were clean white shirts together with sparkling clean white sheets; all whites were pegged out to dry.

My mother picked up my small plastic spade, delved it into the bucket to dig out some sloppy mud. Raising her arm, she tiptoed and stretched upwards and hurled it over the hedge and onto the white washing. She did this again, repeating her actions until the bucket was empty. We all stared. My mother then walked back into the house as if nothing had happened. Of course, my father was out of the house, at work. He had known nothing about this until the next day when there was a knock on the front door. He opened it to see the man from next door.

Mr Smith explained to my father what had happened to his wife's washing. On closing the door, Dad realised there was something radically wrong with my mother. I could hear Mum and Dad talking quietly. Mum explained that a voice in her head had told her to splash the mud onto her neighbour's washing. A voice inside her head! What? Dad suggested she saw a doctor, but my mum dismissed this and just went about her everyday life.

Another bit of weird and wonderful with my mother was that she kept two handbags. She had one for everyday use and another that was duck egg blue and more posh looking, which she used for best. Inside her everyday handbag she had started a collection of objects. Mum kept a pair of sharp scissors, then a small smooth pebble. A pebble, you may ask. What is the significance of a pebble? When asked, she said that someone had hit her over the head with it, so she had kept it so she could hit them back.

As young girls, we would often play with Mum's handbags and would turn out the contents quite frequently, like little girls do. The next addition to her handbag was a small kitchen knife. Us sisters thought it was strange, but I don't think we mentioned it to our father.

More strange behaviour from Mum happened. Whenever somebody knocked on the door, our mother became visibly frightened. She placed a finger over her lips, as if to say 'hush'. Quietly, she beckoned us to move underneath the dining table. We automatically obeyed her. She then hid herself behind the door so that, if the person looked in through the window, she could not be seen. Of course, our father was out at work. He never witnessed this.

Slowly, over the months—this was about 1964—my mother's behaviour changed even more. On a Saturday, she liked to smarten up her appearance so she could venture into town on the bus. My mother preferred to go alone so that she could have a look around and perhaps do a bit of shopping. I suppose she just wanted to have some time alone, to be away from the house and the kids.

I can quite understand that way of thinking. Us girls would be playing on the driveway then watch her walk down the road to the bus terminus. Whereupon she would board the bus, which would take her into the city centre. She did this ritually most Saturdays.

On one occasion, I decided I would like to go with her. Yes, me, Julie. I asked her whether I could go. She immediately replied, 'No.' I begged her. She walked off and I followed her. Halfway down the road, she stopped and told me to go back home. I would not do what she had asked me to do. I was a stubborn child. Once I had had the 'bit' between my teeth, I would go on and on until I got what I wanted. Mum knew this. So when I insisted on going, she relented. We boarded the bus and travelled into the city.

Mother would often visit a large shop called Burtons, which was situated just behind the big Council House on the Old Market Square. Inside, she would shop for bacon, cheese and other things. Burtons, at this time, was like Harrods in London. It boasted of being a purveyor of quality foods. The shop was gloriously set out with beautiful stalls. My mother thought their bacon was the best and the tastiest in town.

Anyway, Mum and I walked around the city. We came upon a clothes shop called Wallis. They had a sale on upstairs. The shop was very busy and people were tightly packed on the stairs. We were reaching the top of the stairs when mother suddenly shouted, 'You tried to push me!' Looking up, I noticed a woman with dark hair replying to my mother. 'No. I did not try to push you, and if I did, I am terribly sorry.'

My mother was repeatedly shouting and became quite distraught. All of a sudden, the manageress appeared. She tried to calm my mother down and ushered us into a side room. My mum started to talk nonsense. The woman soon realised she obviously had mental health issues. The next thing I remember was being taken to the police station in a police car. I can still recollect being inside the Central Police Station. It was cold and uninviting. Mum was questioned. We were then driven home by a female police officer.

The policewoman arrived at our home and we hopped out of the police car. She knocked on our front door, whereupon my father opened the door. The woman indicated she wanted to talk to Dad, preferably inside the house. My sisters and I were told to go and sit on the stairs in the hall.

The adults were in deep conversation. They were in the room for a while, when suddenly, my mother started to scream and shout. Eventually, the policewoman emerged and was walking out of the door. My mother shouted, 'Prostitute! You are a prostitute!'

All of this made it clear to my poor dear father that his wife had become mentally ill. At the time, in Jamaican culture, this type of illness was considered to be shameful. It was a taboo subject. Some people did not like to acknowledge that a family member was suffering in this way. On the island, family members would try to cover it up by saying the person had a brain tumour, or suchlike.

# Chapter Twenty-Five

In the 1960s, people who became mentally ill were assessed and put into special hospitals for psychiatric illness. There was no such thing as Care in the Community in those days. On Porchester Road, just off Mapperley Plains, there was such a hospital called Mapperley Hospital, or 'Mapperley Madhouse', as it was locally known.

One day, in the springtime, a taxi pulled up outside our house. My father opened the front door. Two men in white coats walked into our living room. They were doctors from the hospital. Dad was very 'matter of fact' in the discussion which concerned my mother. My father didn't usually show his emotions in everyday life. He seemed very strong-minded and a little distant. Or was he indeed strong-minded, I ask myself. Perhaps he put his emotions to one side for the duration and refused to feel anything at all.

Thinking about it, he had just lost his son Christopher and now this had happened. My father had to be strong and stay strong for the sake of us children. If Dad broke down, he'd be unable to go to work and provide for his family. Also, us four sisters would have to be taken into care by the intervention of social services. My father had to be clinically cold and distant to preserve his sanity. He could then 'hold everything together' and life would carry on. He was a Jamaican man who had to be seen as strong and proud.

Anyway, back to the story of my mother and the men in white coats. The men explained to Mum that she needed to go to hospital. But Mum would not comply with what the doctors wanted. She protested and cried, 'Who will look after the children?' She was ranting and raving and became highly distraught.

I remember my mother being put into a strange white jacket kind of thing, which looked a bit odd at the time. I later discovered this to be a 'straightjacket'. The jacket held the arms tightly to the body so that the person was held straight, and the arms were bound to the body so there were no flailing arms. Mother became even more agitated. She screamed, 'Let me go. I am not going anywhere!' Then she burst into tears.

The two doctors, one at each side, escorted her through the front door, down the garden path and into the waiting taxi. They took her away to Mapperley Hospital. We sisters just stared out of the window and watched as the taxi disappeared down the road.

The weeks passed by. Dad continued to work hard down the coal mine. My elder sister assumed the role of 'mother'. She was only 11 years old. I remember her cooking a meal of mashed potato, fish fingers and peas one lunchtime. After lunch, she put us to bed for our afternoon nap. She must have remembered our mother doing this and just copied her. It must have been school holiday time. I remember this vividly.

The household then became chaotic. There was never any food in the cupboard. One lunchtime, we were all there, us four sisters. Our eldest sister took some flour from a cupboard. In another cupboard she had found one egg. The milkman had delivered the milk in the morning, so we at least had some milk. A batter mixture was made. This was the mixture for Yorkshire pudding, something she had seen our mother make on a Sunday.

She then suggested I should sneak into the next-door neighbour's garden to 'pinch' some apples from their apple tree. I was frightened although we could see the neighbour's car was missing from the driveway, so we knew nobody was likely to be at home.

Stealthily, I walked to the front paved area of our house and dropped down one step onto the neighbour's path. I clicked open the side gate, which led to the back garden. Climbing the steps to the lawn was easy.

The apple trees spread their branches and I could reach the apples from where I stood. Quickly and nervously, I frantically pulled apples off the tree and hurled them over the privet hedge. My sister was waiting on the other side to scoop them up and take them inside the house. We all knew it was wrong to steal, but we had no choice. We were hungry.

Back in the kitchen, my sister peeled and cored the apples, cut them into thick slices then submerged them into the batter. She then fried them in a large frying pan. So, apple fritters were our lunch for the day! This was the only food we had eaten all day. As I said before, we often went to bed hungry. I think my father thought we were having school dinners, but this was not the case.

I don't think it was deliberate that there was very little food in the cupboard. My father was not able to fetch the groceries due to his long hours at the coal mine. In those days, most grocery stores would be closed at half past five in the afternoon. Petrol stations didn't sell groceries either. There was no twenty-four-hour shopping, as there is today. Dad would rise early in the morning and wouldn't be back home till six o'clock in the evening. So, things became a little dysfunctional. Things were tough for my father and us girls…

# Chapter Twenty-Six

My three sisters and I would often walk up to Mapperley Hospital to visit our mum. The best time to go would be after teatime. I remember the local vicar from our Sunday School at the church down the road becoming involved. He had obviously heard of our mother's hospitalisation.

The clergyman drove an old battered Volkswagen Beetle car. Once he zoomed up Nordean Road to our house and asked whether we would like a lift to the hospital. We accepted and all piled into the small cramped car. He came into the hospital to visit our mum, offering his help and I think he wanted it to be a regular thing. The next time, we refused his lift, preferring instead to walk on our own.

Our dad would sometimes take us all in his car, when he wasn't at work. As I have explained before, in Jamaican culture, mental illness was not acceptable at the time. It was thought of as something to be ashamed of and not talked about. It was thought of as 'bad vibes' and 'spirits' taking over the human body. My father never talked about Mum and her illness. It was just accepted by us sisters that she was in hospital and would probably be better one day.

We heard mother had had electric shock treatment performed in the hospital. It was a very controversial method of treatment at the time.

The patient would be strapped onto a special bed. An injection, to relax the muscles, would be given. Electrical wires would be placed onto the forehead at strategic points. I suppose they were called electrodes. A cloth or 'chew bite' would then be put into the mouth. A certain voltage of electricity would be administered to the patient. This type of treatment was called ECT, or electroconvulsive therapy. The purpose would be to make the bad memories disappear.

I suppose the memories of Christopher dying would be lessened, therefore making it a little bit easier for my mother to cope with her daily life. She was prescribed lithium tablets to take on a daily basis. Mum would then visit a local clinic—not at the hospital—for her monthly injections of some medication. Her mental health would be monitored here.

My dear father was suffering too. I remember his personality seemed to change. He became 'distant'—still 'upbeat,' but distant. He was no longer affectionate towards us, except for the occasional warm smile. Basically, he became a distant, angry man. For example, when one of us sisters was tidying the dinner table and a cup would fall to the floor accidentally, he would react badly.

His shouting was horrendous... 'What have you done! You stupid-looking little devil!' his angry voice boomed. My legs would shake with fear and I would cry. I became frightened of my father whenever he was around. I knew I had to tread carefully.

When any of us sisters asked a question, like 'where should I put this...?' he would, sometimes, fly off the handle with complete and utter rage. I say 'sometimes' because other times you could ask a question and he would be perfectly fine in his response. So, it was like treading on eggshells being around him. You never knew exactly where you stood.

As an older woman now, I truly understand the way my father was. On reflection, he had to cope with the loss of his son,

Christopher. His lovely tall, elegant wife had completely broken down and ended up hospitalised. She was now a mere shadow of her former self. I suppose all of his dreams and hopes of a loving family were now shattered. Who did he have to turn to...?

His Jamaican friends became wary of him for having an emotionally unstable wife. Most kept away for fear of 'catching' the mental illness, for fear of the 'bad spirits' following them perhaps. But my father, too, kept his distance. He must have felt the shame. The shadow of his affected wife was always with him. His friends all knew the story and they were sorry, but they wouldn't talk about it. In the 1960s, things were hardly ever discussed. 'Just sweep it under the carpet. Pretend it never happened.'

There was now a distance between my father and mother. After her spell in hospital, she returned home. The hospitalisation was as long as six to eight weeks. There was hardly any real conversation between Mum and Dad. When they did talk, or ask each other a question, they would sometimes end up arguing. Dad with his booming voice...

My mother would occasionally be withdrawn and quiet then, but on a different day, she would be singing along to the songs on the radio. My mother was well enough to prepare a dinner every day and was fond of cooking one-pot meals using her pressure cooker. Her rabbit stews were scrumptious. Her dumplings were amazing!

Meanwhile, at my father's workplace, a dispute occurred. This was at the Gedling Colliery. My dad had had some training in explosives. He was now a qualified shotfirer and acquired a shotfirer's certificate. There was an opportunity to become a deputy. This meant he would be in charge of a team of coalface workers. He was chosen to apply for the position along with two or three others. His work had been good, also his timekeeping and he'd hardly ever had any days off work. His dedication to the job and willingness to work overtime put him in a highly regarded position. After an interview, the managers gave him the job as deputy.

Well, when the news spread among the workers, they all 'downed tools'. They said they were not having a black man in charge of them. Now, the trade union became involved, the National Union of Mineworkers. A meeting took place at the colliery. The majority of the mine workers had voted against my father to be in charge of them. They wouldn't start work again until the matter was sorted out.

So, the managers put their heads together, so to speak, and decided to phone around the other collieries. At the Bilsthorpe Colliery, the workers were asked whether they objected to a black man being their deputy. They were all fine about it. It didn't matter to the Bilsthorpe men whether he was pink or blue.

My dear father was transferred to the Bilsthorpe Colliery, which was not too far away. He worked as a deputy for the rest of his mining life, which was fifteen years.

# Chapter Twenty-Seven

Dad became an even more angry man. I suppose the bereavement must have made him feel like life was against him. The racial prejudice at the colliery didn't help matters, either. So, it all manifested itself into an emotion far too big for him to comprehend, thus justifying his occasional outbursts in the family.

Almost every day, the prejudices were there for our family. It might be just a 'look' from a white person. A look which suggests you are scum. Going to a local shop, the assistant would sometimes be off-hand with you and brusque. When you asked where to find an item in a shop, the man or woman would say things like, 'Oh we've sold out of that.' Or another assistant would short-change you deliberately to see whether you had noticed. A snide remark would be said about 'gollywogs' or 'black bastards' when you passed by in the street.

It was all colour prejudice and although Mum and Dad tried to ignore it, it was there and so the anger blew up in my father. Mum just retreated into melancholy. My mother was always in and out of hospital most of her married life. When she came home, she would play the dutiful housewife.

I remember, every Sunday she would cook in her kitchen. The radio would be set to Radio 1. This station played all the modern current hits and pop songs. There was a song called 'Everyone's Gone to the Moon'. It was sung by a duo called Chad & Jeremy and it always made her cry. I remember being outside in the garden. I would happen to glance up at the kitchen window only to see my mother with tears rolling down her cheek as the song played.

My mother could never cope much after Christopher died. She never took part in anything happening at our junior school. She never really talked to the neighbour again; except she would say a brief good morning or hello whenever they passed on the street. Although there were some young mums across the street who had children, she only made an effort once or twice to stop and chat when collecting us girls from our school.

Mum would come back into the house and 'mull over' the conversation, decide they were being 'funny' with her, then would say that she didn't like them. She would not engage in friendly conversation ever again. She would just say hello and walk on. Mother would also say something like, 'She gave me a funny look' or 'She gave me a dirty look.' So Mum became a little bit withdrawn and suspicious socially.

One or two old friends would visit us and she would make a pot of tea and pass the time of day. On some occasions, my father would take my mum to visit an old friend and she would be compliant.

I think, really, my mum could not cope with any type of relationship. She failed to really 'connect' with us girls as we were growing up. I suppose you could ask any of my sisters their view on this, whether they 'got on' better with Mum more than I did. Perhaps it was just her relationship with me. She never hugged me or consoled me when I cried; she would just stare and appear not to have real empathy.

I always saw her as a 'distant' mother. Maybe it was the treatment she'd had when hospitalised. The ECT drummed out her ability to feel emotion, maybe. Her occasional liveliness would be apparent whenever she sang to the music on the radio but would not be there otherwise. My mother and father also would not show public displays of affection in the home. I only saw my father embrace my mother once, in the kitchen, soon after Christopher died.

Mum's failure to connect with her children soon manifested itself as also not wanting to connect with her husband. She moved my single bed into their bedroom and told me I had to sleep in Dad's bedroom. Dad slept in his double bed and I slept in my single bed in the same room. I thought at the time the arrangement was bizarre but didn't question it. Mum slept in the back bedroom, in a single bed, while my two sisters shared the double bed, all in the same room. My elder sister had taken over the small single room at the front of the house. John was older and had left home.

My father had accepted this; Mum was talking crazy talk and he just laughed at her and found it all very humorous. There was nothing sinister about sharing a bedroom with Dad. I felt perfectly safe. He would get out of bed at around five o'clock in the morning to go to work down the coal mine. So he was gone by the time eight o'clock came around, when I would get up out of my bed to get ready to go to school. The arrangement didn't last for long—a couple of months maybe.

I remember my mum's sister would visit us. Her husband, Uncle Roy, would ride up Nordean Road on a motorbike with a side car attached to it. My Aunt Marie would sit in the sidecar. The motorbike and sidecar were very popular to be seen on the road in the 1960s, in England. They visited only occasionally. The sisters never really got on well together. It had always been a difficult relationship.

Her sister lived near the Mapperley Hospital where my mum was hospitalised for a few weeks here and there. She was able to work in the hospital and would often pop into the ward where mum was to visit her. But Mum was very uncommunicative and sometimes would not want to see her and would just walk away.

So it's sad they never saw eye to eye. I suppose Mother's illness had got in the way, possibly.

# Chapter Twenty-Eight

In Britain, in 1965, the Race Relations Act was passed through Parliament. It was legislation to address racial discrimination, the first of its kind.

My father came back from the Bilsthorpe Colliery to work as a shotfirer deputy at the Gedling Colliery.

Eric, a fellow Jamaican, and his wife, who was a white woman, would often visit our home. They were old friends. His wife appeared very kind. She had a warm smile. Nell was a down-to-earth, wholesome sort of person. She would enquire about you in a thoughtful way, gently spoken, with no airs or graces.

My father and Eric would sit and discuss racial issues, politics and current affairs. Dad was an intelligent man and would put his point of view over eloquently. Sometimes, the discussion would become quite heated when they disagreed. My father would raise his voice to state his point of view. He would be stubborn and stick to his guns, to what he believed in. When it seemed they would come to blows in disagreement, Eric would bring his sense of humour into the mix and just laugh it off so to dissipate the situation. Then they would both end up laughing together.

My father and mother would often visit Eric and Nell, too, at their house. It was easy for Dad because he drove a car. Eric hadn't learned to drive until later on in life.

In the 1960s, Nottingham City Council began to know of Eric Irons. He had represented many black people regarding racial issues and work-related disciplinary meetings. Eric became involved in racial injustice. He attended many meetings and fought for his fellow Jamaicans when asked to represent them. Whenever there was an issue in the workplace or in the magistrates' court, Eric would be called for his knowledge and expertise on the law. English people on committees and in places of authority began to know of him and respected him. So, eventually, he was asked whether he would like to consider being a Justice of the Peace and sit in the magistrates' court. Eric accepted. He was given an office to work from, situated in the Exchange Arcade, just behind the big Council House in Nottingham's market square.

I remember Dad saying that there had been an accident at Gedling Colliery. He was working alongside fellow miners. Suddenly, there was an almighty rockfall. The man standing next to him was his friend. My Dad stood upright unscathed. His friend was killed.

In the weeks following, my father invited the friend's wife and children round to our house for tea. Her husband had been a fellow Jamaican. I remember everything so vividly. It was a warm summer day in July. All us children did cartwheels on the back lawn, for we had a huge back lawn to play on. We also played a game of rounders...

As there were a large number of children—there were four of us girls and his friend's wife had five or six of her own children—we were seated at the dining table on a rota basis. The tea comprised lettuce, ham, boiled eggs, tomatoes, spring onions and Heinz salad cream. The dessert was a Bird's Trifle or tinned peaches topped with tinned Fussell's cream.

# Chapter Twenty-Nine

I remember when my brother John was 15 and still living at home. He had a group of friends around the house one summer evening. They were drinking cider in the back porch, alongside the kitchen. Anyway, Dad found them and was enraged by the sight of the drunken teenagers. My father shouted at them with his booming voice. He told all of John's friends to go home. Then, he gave John a good thumping.

After this particular incident, and many others, John decided it was time to leave home. Dad had embarrassed him in front of his friends and that was not good. You see, my Jamaican father was a bit too strict. Perhaps, really, he should have just laughed it off. It was probably the first time our John had drunk alcohol. He was also in the safety of his own home.

Soon afterwards, John did leave home. He had found a bedsit to live in, in West Bridgford, a more central part of Nottingham. A local supermarket called Fine Fare was recruiting young school leavers to be apprentice butchers. John filled in an application form and was accepted onto the course.

John was chatty and naturally friendly. He was tall—six feet—and had grown to be a handsome young man. His hair was dark, thick and curly. He had grown a long moustache that stood smartly on his top lip, which was trendy at the time. Remember, this was the 'swinging sixties'. He would listen to music like Tamla Motown. A song called 'Green Onions' by Booker T. & the MGs was one of his favourites. At the

weekend, he would visit a place for young people called The Boat Club, or the Union Club, which could be found along the banks of the River Trent. It was THE place to be seen in; they played all of the popular soul music and Tamla Motown. Major recording label soul and Motown artists visited and played.

Anyway, John was living his life. My dad and John didn't really have a close relationship. Indeed, as far as I know, Dad had never talked, in depth, to John about Christopher's death. Remember, it was John who ran down the road to the telephone box to dial 999, thus summoning an ambulance to the house. It was too late; his brother had died. After all, they were two brothers together. They had formed a close bond as youngsters. I would go as far to say they were soulmates. Two brothers in a family of four sisters.

Our John was a teenager when Christopher died. An age where a boy starts to feel like a man. The hormones raging, a confusing time. He must have been going through an enormous amount of anxiety. But, it seems, John had no one close to talk to. His mother had been hospitalised. His father was distant and angry. There was only one relative, Aunt Marie. I knew there was one time when John had gone to her house and asked to stay for a while because he wasn't getting on well with my father. Aunt Marie said she didn't have the space in her house. She had a daughter and two sons of her own. I know she genuinely didn't have anywhere for him to stay.

So John found a bedsit for himself and duly left home. He had fallen in with a literary group of intellectuals in the city and started to write his own poetry. There, he had made many friends and found a girlfriend. I cannot remember her name. She was a university student and from a good family. Anyway, she took John home to meet her parents and afterwards they told her to stop seeing him. Shall I tell you the reason why? Or can you guess? Yes! It was because he was the son of a black man. His girlfriend had told him so. He wasn't English enough, therefore her white father rejected him. Probably even without getting to know John as a person. For he was a decent guy. John was friendly, with a good sense of humour. A calm and sensitive person was he.

John was maturing and suffering setbacks. I suppose he was starting to feel that life was against him. He had begun to discover the ideals of Martin Luther King. He read books like *Another Country* by James Baldwin.

In the summer of 1967, there was a knock on the door of our home in Woodthorpe. A middle-aged woman stood there, saying she was John's landlady, Mrs Papp. She said she had some news about John.

As she entered the living room and sat down, I noticed she was wearing open-toed sandals, which exposed extremely dirty feet.

She explained to Mum and Dad that John had tried to kill himself. She said he hadn't got up for work as usual. She thought it strange. Later the same day, she grew concerned that she had heard no movement from his room. After knocking on the door a few times, and to no avail, she decided to take matters into her own hands. Mrs Papp had a master key to his room. She opened the door to find John slumped on his bed, seemingly asleep.

At the side of the bed, on the table, there were a load of tablets and bottles of alcohol, some spilt on the floor. Immediately, she phoned for an ambulance. He had been rushed to hospital and had his stomach pumped and was now a patient at the Saxondale Hospital for psychiatric patients.

After Mrs Papp left, my mother burst into tears. Dad mumbled something like, 'That stupid John! What has he done now?'

Dad carried on as normal, not even bothering to visit John in hospital. He would say things like, 'John is a disgrace. That boy will never make anything of himself.'

I think my father probably didn't know how to deal with the situation. He just 'washed his hands of him' (a Jamaican saying). Also, the cultural stigma of mental illness, embedded inside of him, was always there.

# Chapter Thirty

My Jamaican father had decided he wanted to retrain, jobwise. So, he quit the pit. He went to study at a local college and eventually passed his City & Guilds qualification in Heating and Ventilating. There was a recruitment drive that involved an emigration package to relocate to Canada. The idea appealed very much to Dad.

There was a firm promise of a job with a house in Montreal, Manitoba or Ontario. Mum and Dad talked about it and I remember Dad being very positive and excited about the possible move. He put the house up for sale and was trying to sort out emigration procedures and travel. It was all systems go. We all really thought we'd be going to Canada to live.

At the last possible minute, Mum became tearful. She started to put doubts in my father's mind. Then, the final worry was 'And what about Christopher? Who would tend the grave? He would be left behind, all on his own, a forgotten grave.' Mum cried buckets at the thought of this. So, in the end, we didn't go.

A change of plan took place: Plan B. After John's short spell in hospital, it had seemed to Dad that John had somehow lost his way in life. So John was summoned back into the fold and was beginning to get on better with Dad. I think, at this time in my father's life, he had tried to make amends. They now talked and were laughing together. It was happy days.

A discussion took place between Dad and John:

'Would you like to run a little family business? There's an off-licence and general grocer's shop for sale in the Hucknall area, what do you say?'

So, talking about all the ins and outs, John agreed and Mother was happy. It was 1968, the house was now sold and we moved to a small shop in the Hucknall area of Nottingham.

The shop itself was 'for sale' at a price of £2,500. The living accommodation above it had to be rented to my father by the owner.

The man who sold the shop was claiming that he'd made a lot of money each week. He showed my father the bookkeeping ledger, which had intimated the business was thriving. In fact, we later found out the figures in the ledger book were a figment of the man's imagination.

My father was so trusting and maybe a little bit naïve in the way people's minds work. Anyway, owning the shop was a complete disaster in many ways.

# Chapter Thirty-One

It was okay at first. Our John had bought an Austin A40, a small delivery van to go to the cash and carry to buy grocery items but also to deliver groceries to customers. John was 'in charge' of the shop. My father gave it to him to try to make a successful business. After the first year, the shop was just 'ticking over' so to speak. Dad decided to go back to work, for he could use his talents better elsewhere and he needed more income for his family.

In the meantime, us girls went to school at the local grammar school and junior school, where we settled in with our new school routine.

In the backyard of our shop, we stored crates of empty fizzy lemonade bottles. Now in those days, customers would bring their empty pop bottles back to our shop, whereupon we would give them money for returning them. It was like an incentive to recycle glassware. The bottles would then be stored in our yard until collection day by the manufacturer.

Little did we know, there were youths climbing up over the tall gate, taking the bottles, then running around to the front of our shop, where we would give them sixpence for the return of each one. Dad and John soon cottoned on to what was happening. Because of this, John decided to put a guard dog in the backyard. There was a breeder of Alsatians just down the road. John drove off in his van to investigate the dog breeder and her dogs.

One morning, I walked down the stairs to have some breakfast. On opening the adjoining door, to my surprise, this bouncy Alsatian pup jumped up to greet me. As his huge paws landed on my chest, I gasped with surprise. This dog was supposed to be a puppy... but he was so big. The pup had a long body. Its legs were tall and lanky with gigantic saucer-size paws. John called out, 'Down boy, down!' It was only six months old and was already such a big dog—and very excitable. John restrained him and locked him up in the kitchen.

At first, my mother objected to the size of the animal and was against having him in the house. Dad was fine with the dog. To placate my mother, they decided to buy an outdoor kennel for the beast to live in. He was chained up, on a long lead, so that he could roam around outside in the yard.

When us girls opened the kitchen window, we called to the dog. He saw us and sprang up, paws on the window ledge, to greet us. The pup had a huge ginger furry head. He was ultra friendly and fussy and his darling brown eyes gazed inquisitively. We all instantly fell in love with the poor animal. We felt so sorry for his confinement outside where the temperature had started to drop when the sun disappeared from the sky. So we swiftly unchained him and brought him inside to our dining room. He nestled down by the side of a roaring fire my dad had made in the fireplace.

Now we had a problem: we would pet and fuss over our new four-legged friend, but John had repeatedly told us not to bring the dog into the house. So he took him back outside and into the yard. He was supposed to be a guard dog. But, when John had gone out for a while, us girls would open the door and let the huge pup back inside. We now took him up to the living room where we pampered and petted him more! Well, that's the one thing you should *not* do to a guard dog! But he remained inside whenever John was not around. We would scoop him up into our arms to cuddle him and spoil him rotten.

We didn't know what to call the dog at first. He was a pedigree Alsatian and possessed a kennel name of Hargret Rivercroft Handel. Apparently, he was descended from a long line of pedigree champion dogs. His ancestors had been shown at the highly acclaimed Crufts Dog Show. John told us his name was simply Handel.

# Chapter Thirty-Two

A couple of years flew by at the shop. My mother was more on an 'even keel' and John was settling into his new way of life. The pub across the road was called The Kings Arms. There was a young crowd that frequented the pub on a daily basis. John fitted in perfectly and found new friends, so it seemed.

He had asked Dad to accompany him to the pub, but Dad refused. My father had become a bit hesitant to socialise—probably because of past experiences and hostility within the workplace. Mum didn't venture out much either, due to her nerves. She had begun to smoke like a chimney. She stayed at home to watch TV. The doctors at the hospital had suggested she should smoke cigarettes to calm her nerves. Everything seemed quite ordinary until one summer night.

I was asleep in my bed and was awoken by loud banging on the downstairs back door. It must have been in the early hours of a Sunday morning. I could hear the sound of my dad's voice. Two policemen were asking for John. Dad came upstairs to wake John and get him out of his bed. He went downstairs in his pyjamas. Us girls woke up, one by one. We crept down the stairs to listen behind the closed door. Mum saw us and ushered us back to bed. The two policemen had told John to get dressed, as they were arresting him. A woman had accused him of rape.

Us girls ventured back down the stairs and sat still, listening intensely. I heard the muffled voices and the sound of my mother crying. We heard the sound of the kitchen tap being turned on and the gush of water filling the kettle. They must have made a cup of tea to help digest the information the police had just told them. After a while, John was taken away.

110

# Chapter Thirty-Three

The next day, we were told of the news. Mum muttered, 'But John wouldn't do that.'

My father was saying things like, 'That John! I don't know what's got into him ...' He was annoyed and spent the day quite angry. He had refused to go to visit John in the police cell, for he was thoroughly ashamed of his son. He could never show his face at the police station. It was downright too degrading for him. You see, reader, my father was a very upright, upstanding citizen, always had been. He had previously been called for jury service when he had lived in Woodthorpe. Neighbours had respected him.

My father was furious at the sequence of events. He could not quite comprehend what had happened to his son John. So, in the afternoon, my mother wanted to go to the police station, to find out of what had happened. She took me with her, because I had asked to go. The dog needed walking, so he came too. The journey was not too far.

There is a snapshot in my 14-year-old mind. I see John sitting behind bars, as in jail. I see a policeman opening the cell door with his keys. Mum entered the cell and sat down to talk.

I was told to sit in the waiting room, near the entrance. I took the dog and walked down the corridor, which took me back to the station's front door. After what seemed a very long time, Mum emerged full of tears. We walked back home in silence.

She couldn't really talk about it to me because I was a young teenager. At home, Mum and Dad talked about what had happened, but they talked out of earshot of us girls, for we were all too young to properly understand.

# Chapter Thirty-Four

Later, was the court hearing, the trial was held at Nottingham County Court. My mother caught the bus into town every day to listen to the evidence. My father had wanted nothing to do with it at all. He just carried on, as if nothing had happened. Eventually, John was charged and sentenced to three years' imprisonment for rape, which he had always denied. He constantly claimed the woman had consented.

The story goes that John had met his friends in The Kings Arms pub. It was a hot summer's evening. They were all drinking alcohol. A mix of male and females decided to travel on the bus to Nottingham to sample the nightlife.

In the early hours of the morning, they all decided to go their own separate ways home. John had asked to walk a young woman back to her house, bearing in mind they'd known each other for weeks as friends. She agreed.

At some stage, they decided to have sexual intercourse. The young woman was married with two kids. Of course, if John had, in fact, forced himself onto the woman, then rightly so, indeed, he did truly deserve the three years in prison as punishment for his crime.

My older sister hung around with the local teenagers. They were saying things like, 'Your brother was "fitted up" by those people in the pub. Also, 'It was racial prejudice because his dad is black...' These local teenagers had brothers and sisters who were in John's friendship group in the pub.

They were saying, 'She's an older woman with two kids. She knew what she was doing...'

At the time, there was a lot of racial abuse thrown at us girls. Whenever we went to the local recreation ground (the rec), the kids—mainly the lads—chanted racial songs like, 'Too many wogs in this country, la la la la...' For example, when our dog was running around and barking, teenagers would shout, 'Hey! Get that wog dog under control' with a great deal of aggression.

I remember sitting on a swing once. A boy rushed up to me, pushing his face close up to mine—as in his nose was nearly touching my nose. He opened his mouth and screamed, 'Why don't you f*** off back to Africa, you bloody n*****.' His voice was full of sheer hatred. His eyes were wide and menacing.

At the time of owning our shop, name-calling us was a common occurrence. Names like wogs and n****** were used and directed at us. Our shop was called 'the wog shop' and our dog was called 'the wog dog'. I personally was subjected to the most hurtful racial abuse at school. In those days, we had to accept it. Us sisters never told my father about the abuse, because it never came up in conversation. We were a family who did very little talking.

I personally would try to ignore the name-calling and just carried on with everything. When I was called abusive names in the classroom, I would cry though. The teachers just ignored it. There was no such thing as political correctness in those days.

This was the 1970s. A lot of white people hadn't accepted the black West Indians and small island people. There were programmes on television like *Love Thy Neighbour*, starring

Alf Garnett. They openly cracked jokes about black people and Pakistanis. Also, *The Black and White Minstrel Show* was all about white men blacking up their faces and having white lips and singing.

This was the era when skinheads were fashionable. The skinheads were a sub culture of teenagers. They were young people who were bored. They went around the streets causing trouble. They went 'Paki' bashing, for example. This meant roaming the streets looking for Pakistani people to terrorise, racially abusing them, and they would sometimes beat them up.

The skinheads walked around the streets in groups, often looking menacing. They would wear swastika shirts, had arm bands and Nazi-style tattoos. They would address each other with a Nazi-style salute.

Skinheads were also known as 'bovver boys' and wore 'bovver boots', otherwise known as Doc Marten boots. They dressed similarly, in a type of uniform of turned up jeans—some with elasticated braces. The boys' hair was closely cropped. Skinhead girls dressed like the boys and wore the same Doc Marten boots and jeans. Their hair was cut short into a crew cut or 'feathered' style. Skinheads tended to live in poor working-class neighbourhoods, alongside Caribbean immigrants. But not all skinheads were racists. Some just liked the fashion and the sense of identity. And the skinheads liked and followed fashionable music, like ska, soul and reggae— Jamaican-based music.

At this time, there was a politician called Enoch Powell. This man was provoking English people to take action against immigrants. In his view, there were too many black people being accepted into the country. He spoke of England being too much of a melting pot of different cultures. His famous

'Rivers of Blood' speech was broadcast around the country. Enoch Powell was a Conservative Party politician. Some of the skinheads would roam around the streets, chanting, 'Enoch, Enoch.'

116

# Chapter Thirty-Five

After the unfortunate episode of John, the off-licence and general store was opened haphazardly. My father would arise early to go to his day job in the factory in Beeston. After working a full day's shift, he would come home, where his evening meal was dutifully prepared by my mother. After a twenty-minute after-dinner snooze, he would then proceed to open up the shop.

It was now Christmastime and the shop was becoming busy in the evening. People were having parties and would come to our shop to buy big party cans of beer. These were very popular, and we were often selling out of them, so Dad had to make frequent trips to the brewery to buy more. It was a fantastic few weeks, in which Dad made an unusually exceptional amount of money. It was a great time. But after the Christmas period was over, it was a different story... Hardly any people visited our shop.

Summertime came and my father soon realised that he was flogging a 'dead horse', so to speak. There were cash and carry bills to pay and he couldn't pay them. There was also rent to pay for the living accommodation. My father decided to close the shop and move out. All of the money from the sale of his Woodthorpe home had now been lost in the shop. There was no money left to buy another property.

So what do you think my dad did? How do you think he solved the problem of homelessness for a family of four daughters and a wife?

Well, he took us to the seaside, on the east coast, to Ingoldmells, near Skegness. He rented an eight-berth caravan.

They were very difficult times indeed. As I've said before, there was hardly any discussion in the family ever. My father made the decisions and we were just told we were going to be doing this or doing that. The furniture in our home above the shop was taken away by removal men and put into storage, as there was no new home to move into. The storage company charged a daily rate, so the bill was piling up every day.

I remember the summer by the seaside. Thinking about it, us girls were oblivious to the severity of the situation. Nobody had mentioned the word 'homeless'. We were happy girls. It was like a little adventure for us.

There was a small fairground in Ingoldmells in a place called Vickers Point. Our eldest sister was 16. She had arranged to see some friends at the fair—for in those days a lot of Nottingham people spent their summer holidays in Skegness or neighbouring seaside towns. So it would be quite common to bump into your school mates at the seaside.

All us sisters were at the fair. I remember just standing by the waltzer. The song of the summer was 'My Cherie Amour' by Stevie Wonder. It was played loudly. Whenever I hear the song now, I think of the waltzer, the fairground and Ingoldmells.

Some rides were fast and daring. The teenage gypsy boys would play dare-devil. With the waltzer whizzing around at speed, they would hop onto the ride, balancing themselves just behind the cars as they were spinning. We all gasped with horror at the thought of them slipping and then dropping down beneath the boards to be crushed and smashed to smithereens. What a sight they were. The gypsy boys would be showing off to all the girls standing around. It was great fun.

In the meantime, my Jamaican father was having a hard time. After installing us in the caravan, he returned to Nottingham. He continued to work at the British Celanese plant in Beeston. At night-time he had no home to go to. He would drive in his car to a lonely side road or country park. There, he would settle down for the night and huddle up in the back seat to sleep.

It was a good thing it was summertime, for at least he didn't have to suffer the cold. In the morning, he would drive himself to work. I suppose the factory had a canteen where he could buy himself a meal. At the weekend, he would then drive to Ingoldmells to enjoy some family time. My dear, dear father battled on, never giving up...

Some weekends he wouldn't show at all and there was no way of letting my mother know. There were no mobile phones and a letter would have taken too long to reach her. So I suppose she just waited. For Dad spent the time trying to find somewhere to live. He had, after all, lost most of his money in the shop venture. He only had his weekly wages to rely on.

The school summer holidays had come to an end. We were still living in the caravan. Children were returning to school for the start of the Autumn term. Stuck at the seaside, in desperation, my father contacted his West Indian friend Eric. He must have telephoned him and told him of his plight.

Eric had contacts in Nottingham and was able to find an empty house. So Dad collected us all from the seaside and promptly installed us in a house on Sherbrook Terrace in Daybrook, Nottingham. The house was an old three-storey terraced property. I remember there was an alleyway which led to a gate and a backyard. In one corner of the yard was an outhouse with a toilet. A cold and uninviting place—without lights at night-time. The house itself was spacious. I remember the rooms being large and roomy.

On entering the back dining room, I recall the bare wires protruding from an electrical open socket high up in the middle of the wall. In my naivety, I took hold of one wire, then with my other hand, I connected it to the other wire. Instantly, there were sparks flying and I was shocked by the surge of electricity. I screamed. My parents realised what had happened and shouted at me for being so stupid. Luckily, I was fine. I think the house had an old-fashioned type of electrical circuit, known as DC electric power, or something...

In fact, the whole house was a bit run-down. There were bare floorboards everywhere. In the front room you had to be careful not to fall into the cellar. There were two floorboards missing along the length of the room, exposing the cellar beneath. Dad managed to replace the floorboards neatly and cover the gap, thus making it safe for us.

There were other minor issues, like a handle missing off a door, so when the door closed you were locked in. A small amount of money was paid to the storage people to release our beds, some bedding and a cooker, but not furniture, wardrobes or clothes. More money would have to be paid later to release the rest of our belongings, for we were poor. The dilapidated house was apparently rent-free. I think a charity had owned it. Dad was not planning for us to stay there for too long...

# Chapter Thirty-Six

The start of the school autumn term had arrived. We had no school uniform to wear. In the rush to vacate the shop, my mother had not sorted the clothes, or probably had not been given enough time. The uniforms were still hanging up in the wardrobe, which was in the removals storage warehouse.

My father had to drive us to school in the first week. It was now a long way to get to school. It involved the use of two buses, with an early start to get there.

When my sister and I arrived at the school in our normal day clothes, we were ushered into the deputy head's office. She was told of our plight and handed us second-hand uniforms to put on. I remember my blouse had another student's name sewn into it. Great. But we had been kitted out and were truly grateful.

Life carried on. My other sisters went to the local junior school, to which they could walk. This was a hard time for them. For to be a 'newbie' in the classroom was painful for them and very stressful. They had to leave the old friends behind and start again.

My father continued to work hard. Because he didn't have to pay rent for a few months, he was able to save a deposit to buy his own house again. I also assume he'd got a bit of money from the sale of the shop, which he had owned. These weren't easy times and every penny had to be accounted for and saved.

In the meantime, it was very difficult for my sister and me to go back and forth to school every day. We had to walk twenty minutes to Hucknall Road, where there was a golf course. We would then catch the number 84 Trent bus to Hucknall Market Place. On reaching there, we would then catch another bus up to the school. It was hard, but we managed it.

There was one time where my father picked us up from school. On the way back to Sherbrook Terrace, we had stopped by at our old shop for him to pick up some mail. Our car was parked in a side road across the road from our shop, near The Kings Arms pub. All us girls were sitting in the back seat. Mother was in the front. Dad had got out of the car to walk across the main road to the shop.

After a while, he came back, clutching his mail to his chest. Once settled in the car, he turned the ignition and was just about to drive off when one of us girls, then all of us, turned to look out of the back window. We saw our dog, Handel, running like mad across the busy main road towards the car. A huge thick chain was trailing behind him. 'Handel!' we all shouted in chorus. Dad waited. We opened our car door and this ginger-headed excitable Alsatian climbed in, nearly smothering us all. He was crying out with joy to see us again. We all laughed and stroked his long furry body. His chain was pulled into the car, from the pavement, and Dad drove the car home.

Apparently, when we became homeless, our lovely dog had been given to a friend, who had chained him up on his allotment by the railway side. He had obviously broken free and made his way back to the shop. It was only down the road, not too far away. I do not know how long he had been roaming around the street, near the backyard of our shop...

We arrived back at Sherbrook Terrace. This time, Handel was with us! My mother let him roam outside in the secure backyard. Every time we came home from school, we would be greeted by Handel, his furry head peeping over the gate. He would climb up to see over it. His huge front paws would be holding onto the top, his head peering out. Oh, such memories! He was so funny and such a joy to us in our enduring circumstances.

Now, our family life was back on track, so to speak. My father would work hard and often also at the weekend. Mum ran the household under great difficulty. She was quite well mentally at this stage in her life.

Our furniture had not been recovered. We managed to live sparsely, with only basic things. The toilet facilities were far from adequate, there being no toilet inside the house. So, in the bathroom, upstairs, my mother had placed a large bucket. This was our toilet in the evening and at night-time, for it was too cold and dark to venture out into the backyard to use the outside loo.

Two of us girls had the chore of taking the full bucket to the toilet in the backyard to be emptied every morning before we went to school. We took it in turns every day to carry out the task. It was always full to the brim—and heavy. It took two of us to lift it. Carefully, we would walk down the stairs, through the kitchen, out of the back door to the outside toilet. The house was obviously in the process of being upgraded. The bathroom had been stripped of the bath and only a small sink stood there to use. That was all.

We stayed at Sherbrook Terrace for about six months. Mum and Dad had started to look in the Hucknall area of Nottingham for a house to buy. Houses were much cheaper here and more affordable. Also, us two older sisters were taking our GCE exams at school, so we had to live nearby.

# Chapter Thirty-Seven

Mum and Dad drove around the neighbourhood near to our school. Along Nabbs Lane were all council houses and at the end, just below the school was a new estate, not brand new, but modern. There was a semi-detached house for sale on Ascot Drive, not too bad an area. My father put down a deposit to secure the purchase, for it was only just affordable. The house was a traditional three-bedroom semi-detached house with driveway and garden—front and back.

For my father was itching to be in a home of his own once again. You see my father was always an optimistic kind of a guy. If any thing or any situation got him down, he wouldn't show it. He would still be upbeat in temperament and from time to time would even burst into song while listening to the radio.

Hucknall in the 70s was a mining community. It was predominantly full of white working-class people. So when our family went to view the house, curtains would twitch from the spying neighbours. When the house purchase was being finalised, my father went to visit the man at the house to talk about which fixtures and fittings he would be leaving. But, when Dad asked about the moving-in date, there was something wrong. The guy couldn't look at my dad's face to begin with. Fidgeting and shuffling his feet, looking very uneasy, he explained to my father about the man across the road. The man opposite didn't like the idea of a black family moving into the neighbourhood. He had swiftly put his house up for sale when he had found out and was waiting to sell—before we moved in!

What a blow to my dear father. Some people are not accepting of black people. They need to find out the character of the person before making judgement and then discriminating. A man is a man, no matter the colour of his skin.

Anyway, there was a delay of a couple of months before we could all move into our new home. The racist man and family still resided across the road, but we ignored them. He was gone after a few weeks had passed by and a new family moved in. We later found out the bigot was in fact working as a policeman...

Mum was happy to have a proper home of her own. She made new curtains, for she was a natural seamstress. Us four girls were teenagers or entering teenage years. Handel, the dog, was an active, very much-loved part of the family.

I remember quite vividly one morning walking to school. My sister and I walked down Ascot Drive, across the road, then onto the school field. As we approached the school, I looked behind to see Handel running as fast as lightning towards us. He had escaped from the house and followed us. He began to bark at all the children passing by. We walked into the paved 'quad' area, the centre of the school, where he followed. Not knowing what to do, we just left him, for he would surely find his own way back home over the field, across the road, up the road, then home. It was funny though.

The family was settled now. Us four daughters would hang around with our friends, our bikes and our dog. Our favourite place was walking in the Misk Hills, alongside the school. It was fields and farmland. In the springtime it was especially lovely. We would all walk with our dog and friends across fields and up hills until we came to a wooded area. It was absolutely laden with the most colourful bluebells. A sheer carpet of blue, it was breathtakingly gorgeous. Of course it was locally known as Bluebell Wood. Here, we came across rabbits hopping around, much to Handel's delight.

As soon as we came out of the wood and back onto the fields, flocks of sheep soon became apparent. On seeing the sheep, Handel started to bark and chase them. He had a loud aggressive bark, in fact quite menacing. The farmer suddenly appeared with his shotgun. He told us to control our dog, otherwise he would shoot him. He kept on saying he had every right to shoot our dog because he was on his farmland and worrying his sheep. So of course, being teenagers, we just 'legged it' and ran until the farmer was out of sight! Happy carefree days, eh!

Meanwhile, back at the house, I noticed my dad was always complaining about the council estate situated just one road away, towards the back of our house. He would say things like, 'Did you see those gangs of teenagers stood at the corner?' and 'Did you hear the language of those young people who have just walked by our house?' Also, we suffered racist taunts. A group of lads stood outside our home one night, chanting songs and throwing stones at our windows. Fortunately, no windows were broken.

Dad wasn't happy with the neighbourhood. Alas, it was not as cultured and peaceful as his beloved Woodthorpe. He was yearning deep down inside to get back to the neighbourhood he had once loved. Because we had lost money in the downtrodden shop, this was the only area of Nottingham we could afford to live in and it was close to our school. My father just had to bide his time.

# Chapter Thirty-Eight

So after about four years, when we had finished our schooling, Dad went sniffing around Woodthorpe again. He had found a better paid job at a Boots warehouse in Ilkeston. The money was good. He was still paid weekly. Most people were paid their wages in cash and had their weekly pay packet presented to them in a small brown envelope at the end of each week.

I can still remember Dad scouring the property section in the *Nottingham Evening Post*, looking for houses to buy. He'd had enough of having to drive through the council estate to get to the main road. It seemed to make him angry and he found this part of the neighbourhood downright utterly depressing. (Sorry, reader, if you do happen to live in social housing.) I know it seems like my father was a total snob, but, reader, when you lived in a better neighbourhood, there was no racial abuse thrown at you. People were better behaved. If they felt racist towards you, they would not express their feelings. At last he had found a detached house, set high up on a hill on Walsingham Road in Woodthorpe.

The house had been drastically reduced in price and was up for sale at ten thousand pounds. The price of a similar house in the neighbourhood was £14,000, by the way, just to tell you how drastically reduced the property was. The house had been repossessed by the mortgage people. So the building society had just wanted a quick sale to recover their money owed by the previous occupants. Apparently, the man and woman who had been living there were going through a marriage break-up.

The house had been emptied and we were able to go and view the property. On walking through the front door into the hall, I noticed a glass pane on the kitchen door had been smashed. More things were broken, but fixable. We all walked into the lounge and could not believe how spacious and smart it was. Mum and Dad were really pleased. Dad ran up and down the stairs, inspecting everything in sheer delight. It was a lovely detached house with a driveway, garage and gardens, front and back, on a corner plot.

So we had moved back to Woodthorpe. Our neighbours were friendly and welcomed us by knocking on our door and presenting us with a bowl of fruit. He was a doctor and she was a housewife with children. We soon settled in and life was good again. Dad would mow the lawns regularly and manicured his garden with perfection. He was indeed proud and happy once more.

# Chapter Thirty-Nine

Us girls were now older and leaving school. I had left school at 16, in 1973, and found work in an office in a civil service department. Dad had suggested I apply for the vacancy he had seen advertised in the local newspaper.

He had told or maybe 'ordered' us to find a 'nice clean' job in an office. Also, to look out for a job with a pension. I didn't know what else to do, so I followed his advice. I was not particularly ambitious and was a quiet, shy person—'a plodder', I suppose. My only aim in life was to find a husband and have children. That was all I thought was expected of me. My sisters all aspired to the same in life as me and they did exactly the same...

It was the school holidays and my younger sisters were at home. I was aware of my mother sitting in her chair in the lounge. Suddenly, she started laughing about what seemed to be no apparent reason. I asked, 'Mum, why are you laughing?'

She replied, 'I'm laughing at my thoughts...'

I just looked away and she repeatedly laughed out loud. This behaviour recurred every week.

She also started to say strange things, like, 'Look here, Julie', pointing at her leg. 'I've got a bullet wound here, from the war. I was shot, you know!'

Whereupon I said to her, 'Mum, are you alright?'

A few evenings later, I shared with my dad what my mother had been saying. He said, 'She hasn't been taking her tablets. She refuses to. I have noticed her strange behaviour. I think someone needs to call a doctor. Can you do that for me?'

I replied, 'Really, shall I phone the doctor?'

He said, 'Here, have some money for the telephone box.' On opening the sideboard door, he hunted around for some loose change.

Immediately, I put on my jacket. He handed me the coins and a piece of paper with the telephone number of the doctor's surgery. I walked out of the door and headed down the road to the telephone box where I phoned the doctor. I happened to speak to the actual doctor. You could in those days and the doctor knew who you were and knew of my mother. I told him my mother had had a relapse and I explained her bizarre behaviour to him. This was about four o'clock in the afternoon.

Later, I had just popped to Mapperley Plains to do some shopping. On walking back onto Walsingham Road, I noticed in the distance an ambulance parked outside our house. That was quick, I thought. My mother had packed a few things into a small suitcase. She was compliant when advised she needed to spend some time in Mapperley Hospital. I saw her climb the ambulance steps and the ambulance was gone in a blink of an eye.

When I entered the house, my father seemed tired and rather complacent about it all. She was gone for a month or so, then returned to the household, accepting of what had happened to her and now 'back to normal'. She seemed to have enjoyed her sojourn. Her eyes were brighter and she appeared to have more of a 'spring in her step'.

# Chapter Forty

My mother had started to talk about John. We hadn't heard from him for a few years now and she was pining for word of him. Obviously, during his spell in prison, he had written frequently to his mother and Mother had written back. A few sparse times she had visited him, but never our dad. After all, in his eyes, it was too shameful to even step foot inside a prison. Dad had kept away.

A few years before, John had written to say he was being released, but he gave no forwarding address. We hadn't a clue what he was doing now or where he was living. He'd lost contact with his family.

One afternoon, I was reading a women's magazine. On reading the problem page, there was a letter written by a mother who had lost contact with her son. She didn't know how to go about trying to find out where he lived. The reply was to contact the Salvation Army Missing Persons Bureau and supply them with the person's National Insurance number and their last known address. There was an address to write to.

Exhilarated, I told Mum. She looked at the magazine article and asked would I write to the Salvation Army? I then raced upstairs to find John's big old rucksack, still full of his belongings. I wondered whether there would be any personal information inside.

On rummaging through his things, I found the following contents: a collection of poetry and short stories. The thoughts written were mainly dark and described death and dying. I suppose he had tried to express his thoughts on Christopher through his written poetry. He, too, had lost his brother.

Another poem about Woodthorpe Park describes the trees in autumn. His rucksack further contained a couple of mouth organs, kept neatly in their original boxes. There were cufflinks, a pipe with tobacco tin, various pens, a hair comb, bottle of aftershave and paperback books.

One was written by Edgar Allan Poe. Another was about cowboys and Indians and the Wild West of America. There were toy cars (possibly belonging to Christopher), a couple of car maintenance books, an address book, with names of girlfriends and their telephone numbers. Lastly, I found a card with his National Insurance number written on it. This was gold, as far as I was concerned...

Almost immediately, I sat down at the dining room table and wrote my letter to the Salvation Army Missing Persons Bureau.

# Chapter Forty-One

Within two weeks we had a letter from the Salvation Army giving John's latest address, which was in Birmingham. Mum was absolutely elated and so was I. Straight away, Mother wrote to John. Very soon, a letter came back. It was amazing how speedy we were all back in touch with each other again. Dad was secretly pleased also because deep down inside he had wondered what had become of his son.

My mother frequently wrote letters. John replied by return of post. After all, there was a lot of catching up to do, as the years had passed by.

John was invited home for Christmas, but he never came. I don't know why. Perhaps he was planning on doing something in Birmingham with loved ones he had found. The letters kept on flowing between mother and son. Occasionally, my mother would let me read some of John's letters. Mainly, she kept them private.

Us sisters were all growing up and marrying or having boyfriends. Things were more settled at home for Mum and Dad. My father, on a Sunday, would wash and polish his car. His car was his prized possession. This time, he drove a Ford Escort, which was the smallest size car he'd ever owned.

One summer, because us girls were all grown up and doing our own thing, my mother and father decided to have a week away on the east coast. They rented a caravan in Ingoldmells, just the two of them. It must have seemed so strange for them, after always having loads of children around them all the time. They didn't really talk to us about what they did or where they visited. As I've said before, our family never really discussed things. They just said they had a nice time.

Anyway, after the holiday, my mother decided not to travel in Dad's car anymore. She had said, 'his driving was bad' and she had become quite frightened.

Dad had taken a trip out to Mansfield to visit my sister, but Mother had not wanted to travel with him. She stayed at home. Whenever I had travelled in his car in previous years, Dad had always seemed to be a bad-tempered driver. Not all the time, but quite often.

On one occasion, while approaching a junction, the traffic lights were on green for go. Dad drove through them then slammed on his brakes to allow a man to walk over a zebra crossing. Unfortunately, as a result, the car behind crashed into the back of Dad's car. As a result, he became cross with the driver. There was an exchange of words that were not very pleasant at the time.

When driving at other times, he would remark, 'Did you see him!' when another driver had done something wrong. Or he would just shout, 'Bloody fool!'

Smile...

# Chapter Forty-Two

I soon turned 18. I had my first real boyfriend. We wanted to go into the city at night to dance. The nightclubs were popular places for young people to visit. Sophisticated places like Intercon were newly opened around the Victoria Centre. Other nightclubs like Madisons, Scamps and the Ad-Lib Club were the new places to visit, or 'hang out'. They usually opened their doors at about nine o'clock in the evening. They were licensed to stay open until two o'clock in the morning. They were places to dance and have a few drinks. Food was served, like 'chicken in a basket'. It felt very grown-up to be out in one of those places! Long evening dresses and high platform shoes were fashionable at the time, along with the big hairstyles. Remember the music from bands like Abba, who were at the top of the music charts.

My Jamaican father had told me I wasn't allowed to come home too late at night. This was very unfair because he didn't register the fact that all nightlife usually ends in the early hours of the morning. He had wanted me to be home at eleven o'clock at night and that was his final word. He would comment that only girls of 'ill repute' stayed out all night... But I was young and vibrant. Dancing and raving all night with my boyfriend or going to see live bands was all I wanted to do. So my father would say, 'The door will be locked at eleven o'clock. Am sorry, but if you're not home by eleven, you will be locked out.'

I came home after an evening out. I had asked my boyfriend to wait in his car while I tried the front door. It was twenty to twelve and guess what, the front door was well and truly locked! The lights were out, and all occupants had retired to their beds. Returning to his car, my boyfriend said the only solution was to go back with him to his mum and dad's house, where he lived. So, this is what happened.

The next day, I got up, got dressed and went to work from his house. At home time, I took the bus home to face my father.

'Where were you last night?' came the booming voice. I explained to him what had happened. Then, my mother joined in the conversation, agreeing with me that he was being unreasonable. My mother continued to try and talk my father around to my way of thinking. But he continued to 'lay down the law', raising his voice even more.

It was like talking to a brick wall with my dad. He didn't seem to have the power of reasoning. As far as he was concerned, his decision was final. So, feeling frustrated, I stormed off upstairs to the solace of my bedroom, feeling really upset.

The same evening, my boyfriend showed up at the door. My father opened the door and they both stood outside arguing. Out of the window, I could see my boyfriend retreating down the driveway and all I could hear was my father's booming voice. Well, I was so upset, I decided to pack a bag and go and live at my boyfriend's house, there and then. So that was that!

Well, about a week later, I was at my office desk at work and the telephone rang. My colleague answered it, then handed the phone to me. I heard a voice on the other end saying, 'Hello, this is the Palais de Danse. You have just won the competition in the beauty contest...' I recognised the voice of my father, and he was laughing. He told me to come home.

The conversation was short. He'd delivered what he had wanted to say, then the telephone call ended, with me saying something like, 'Alright, Dad.'

This kind of cranky behaviour, about coming home on time after a night out, had happened to all my sisters, just the same with their boyfriends.

So, with my few possessions. I moved back home.

I was just thinking… This must have been quite a big thing for Dad to pick up the telephone, to dial the number and then actually talk to me. You see, he didn't like the telephone. Growing up in a world without gadgets, he found the telephone quite bizarre in that there was this voice, I suppose, in 'mid-air'… not attached to anything or anyone.

A year ago, when we first had a phone installed in our home and it rang, he would always ask my mother to answer it. If she was upstairs or out, he would have no choice but to pick it up.

He would become quite muddled talking to the voice at the other end, the person he couldn't see. He would hold the receiver in bewilderment. He couldn't fathom out the timing concerning when to speak, the rhythm of the conversation, when to pause.

He would often end up just putting the phone down in despair. You see, the telephone was new to him; he had hardly ever used one before. But later on, in time, he did get to grips with it all… Smile.

# Chapter Forty-Three

My father had always painted and decorated his own house and would wear his old navy blue boiler suit. It was a protective garment so keeping his trousers and shirt clean, which he wore underneath. Every day, he would wear a clean shirt and smart trousers, never blue jeans nor T-shirt. I suppose it was his generation to wear smart clothes, dating back from the war years.

It seemed like he quite enjoyed stripping off wallpaper, the cleaning of a wall, then, of course, the actual paperhanging. He didn't always get it perfect. Sometimes, you could see the occasional overlap. But it always looked alright and indeed he did improve the look of a room.

Dad would always complete his decorating within a few days. Like, he would start to decorate a room on a weekend and work hard at it all day. He would only stop for a bite to eat at lunchtime, or to drink the occasional cup of tea. My mother would help him hold a piece of wallpaper. Mostly, she would busy about her housework or start baking in the kitchen.

All of the houses my father ever owned were kept to a good standard of maintenance. Any repairs to chimney pots, gutters etc. were done straight away. He mostly preferred to employ qualified tradesmen to fix things, especially for any repairs to guttering or chimney pots, which were high up towards the roof of the house.

You see, my father was afraid of heights. Being indoors on a stepladder was okay for him, but when it came to be climbing longer ladders outside, he wouldn't climb them. He explained that he felt a little bit 'wobbly' and unsteady when it came to heights. My father could always afford to pay the tradesmen and was proud to do so. The house was always kept 'shipshape and Bristol fashion'. The outside gardens were trimmed, clipped and neat. My father especially liked roses.

In fact, he would order rose plants from a reputable rose grower from as far away as Scotland. He would prepare the ground for planting beforehand. The hole would be dug and a handful of bonemeal would be thrown in with a spadeful of local farm manure. Then he would delicately place the rose plant into the hole, then fill the hole in with good solid earth. The rose seller's label would be clearly displayed with pride. He would then clip, prune and nurture his rose plants all year round. At the right time of year, he would vigorously prune them so that the following year, the rose would produce some lovely strong blooms. He particularly would choose the highly scented variety. These he would cut and bring into the home for my mother to place into vases.

His lawn was neatly cut with his beloved lawnmower and clipped to perfection. After cutting the lawn, he would then oil, grease and sharpen the parts on his hand-driven push machine.

When the electric lawnmower became fashionable, Dad would always prefer to keep his little old mower, which he had used for the last fifteen years or more. He would walk up and down, back and forth with it. I suppose his mower was less noisy than the new electric ones and it must have therefore been quite therapeutic for him. The walking up and down the lawn, the fresh air, the tranquillity of the peaceful garden...

# Chapter Forty-Four

My father was regimented about the time he would go about his day. I mean, for example, he had to arise at six o'clock in the morning, obviously to be able to go to work on a week day. At the weekend, he would always get out of his bed at around nine o'clock. He would never lie in bed being idle. Also, I had only once seen him ill in bed in my whole lifetime. He was rarely ill. Okay, he might have the occasional headache, for which he would perhaps take two Anadin tablets with water.

His favourite breakfast would be a bowl of hot porridge oats, eaten with a little milk and some sugar sprinkled on top. The milk would always be sterilised milk from a glass bottle. With the porridge he would drink one cup of tea. Sometimes, he would prepare a slice of toast. He would then spread Stork margarine and perhaps a little marmalade or Marmite on the top.

At the weekends, maybe he would eat a cooked breakfast— usually bacon, eggs, fried bread, tomatoes and baked beans. Mid-morning, he would make himself a cup of tea or coffee. It was rare for him to have a snack. If he did, it would be a couple of biscuits—probably digestives or a piece of fruit cake—and just eat one slice only.

My father would always look at his wrist-watch and announce, 'Oh it's one o'clock. Time for lunch.' Rigidly, one o'clock on the dot! I suppose his timings came from his days in the military. Discipline can often stay with a person for the rest of their lives.

So, at one o'clock, he would eat a bread sandwich and have a cup of tea. Maybe have an apple or an orange. Later in the afternoon, my father would drink a cup of tea or coffee and eat nothing. He wasn't really a 'snack' person, nor was he a soft drinks person. Only very occasionally, in the summer, he would have a glass of orange squash. He only drank tea, coffee, water, hot cocoa, Ovaltine, or the occasional beer.

Again, rigidly, at six o'clock in the evening, my mother would have an evening meal prepared. The family would sit down together and eat. Later, at suppertime, maybe he would eat a few crackers and cheese and enjoy a cup of cocoa or similar.

He would mostly retire to his bed around half past ten or eleven o'clock. Sometimes, on a Saturday night, he would stay up to watch a late-night film on the television.

The British fish and chip shops were the only type of takeaway food at the time, in my dad's era. In the late 70s, Chinese takeaways were only just beginning to come into fashion on the high street. So Dad would eat the occasional fish and chips and mushy peas takeaway. He never enjoyed a Chinese meal. He would say, 'They are all rubbish.'

Neither would he eat junk food or overprocessed foods. He just ate natural foods which haven't been messed about with. I suppose 'basic' food.

When he drank alcohol, it would always be at the weekend. That could be one or two small bottles of beer, never more. Later in life, he would like to drink red wine with his evening meal. He preferred red wine. He'd only drink a couple of glasses though.

At Christmastime, he would treat himself to a bottle of his favourite Lamb's Navy Rum. Again, he would indulge in only one or two glasses. His favourite Christmas drink was rum and black (blackcurrant juice). One of my father's sayings and pearls of wisdom was, 'Your body is your temple. Be careful what you put into it...'

He was not a regular 'pub' man either. The only pub I ever knew he frequented was Yates's Wine Bar, situated in the Nottingham city centre, just off the Old Market Square. This was far back in the 60s. Even then, he only went out a few times to meet up with old RAF friends.

My parents rarely went out in the evening. They were content to stay at home and watch the television. I suppose they were just homely people. Their generation often would stay indoors for entertainment. This wasn't unusual.

# Chapter Forty-Five

At the time, I myself was living in a bedsit within a shared house in the Sherwood area of Nottingham. I regularly visited my mother and father—every three weeks or so. There was often one or more of my sisters there and we would all have a pow-wow together.

On this occasion, I had left the visit for much longer: about five weeks. When I arrived at the front door, I knocked. Usually our dog, Handel, would bound up to the door and bark ferociously. I would hear him frantically sniffing, knowing his nose would be pushed against the bottom of the door. But this time it was extremely quiet. My mother opened the door. As I stepped in, I whispered, 'Where's Handel?' I walked into the lounge, taking off my hat and coat. Now seated in her chair, she nonchalantly replied, 'He's died.'

I immediately burst into tears. Bewildered, I exclaimed, 'Well, why didn't you tell me? You could have phoned me at work!' The tears rolled down my cheeks. I sat down, and my father walked into the room. Settling into his armchair, he told me he thought our dog had been poisoned. 'What makes you think that, Dad?'

He explained that he would let him out in the evening to run up the street and back. (In those days, people would just let their dogs out to roam. There were no laws about dog mess either.) My parents apparently never walked the dog. This was because Handel was not obedient on his lead. He was a strong

Alsatian and he pulled my mother and father over, so they would just let him out to roam.

He explained that our dog would rummage in the waste-bins at the big house up the road. He had tried to stop him from doing this, but he would always end up where the bins were and make quite a mess (in those days there were no huge wheelie bins. The bins were half the size, usually made of metal 'tin' with a loose-fitting lid on the top.) It was easy for a large dog to knock the bin over and pick over the contents.

My father would go to the house to apologise and would tidy up the mess. But it was always a problem. He let him out to roam one afternoon and Handel had come back home. Dad had found him sitting down outside the front door, finishing off some meat he had found. A few days later he became ill. He could hardly walk and his back legs wouldn't support his body. Then suddenly he passed away.

Then mother chimed in and said, 'Well, Handel was sleeping a lot. In the afternoon, he couldn't walk very well. He was unsteady on his feet.'

Now Dad would arrive home from work at exactly five o'clock each working day. Mum said that Handel always waited at the door, ready to greet him. On that day, when Dad came home and made a fuss of him, the dog simply stumbled into the kitchen, lay down on the floor and died.

It had seemed like he had especially waited for his master to come home, probably knowing he was going to die… As if greeting him for the very last time. Of course, my parents were very upset.

I asked what he had done with Handel after his passing. He explained he had lifted him up, staggering under the weight, then placed him in the boot of the car and taken him to the vet's on Woodborough Road not too far away.

In those days, there were no vet's fees for disposing of animal bodies—as there are today. Also, very little in the way of sentiment. You could simply take your dead animal to the nearest vet to be disposed of. The bodies would be collected by a glue merchant. Animal bones were turned into glue, apparently. Hardly any sentimental cremations, no fees, no nothing.

Or pet owners could simply bury their animals in their own back garden. So, I suppose with our dog, being such a huge animal, my father didn't like the idea of having to dig such a deep hole. I think it must have been far easier to take the dog to the vet—like he did.

# Chapter Forty-Six

Apparently, one summer's day, there was a knock on the door. When my father opened it, there stood our John, with a blonde woman. He announced her as his wife and her name was Jane.

Of course, my mother had regularly written to him, and he regularly wrote back, but no mention of any wife, until she arrived at our door. It was indeed a big surprise to see John and Jane. As usual, John was holding a big box of chocolates and presented them to my mother as he and Jane entered our house.

At this time, I had returned home to live with my parents and I remember the look of surprise on my mother's face. Jane was friendly and spoke with a Birmingham accent. John had also picked up the accent...

They explained their small register office wedding. They seemed happy enough. My father and John chatted away amicably. I have to say, John had driven up from Birmingham in an old Daimler, classic car. He took my father outside to see it. He was excitable showing the lovely walnut dashboard, the luxurious leather seats. It was a traditional classic car, which he treated with pride and joy. This was indeed a happy event. They stayed over for one night, then swiftly travelled back to Birmingham.

Soon afterwards, John and Jane decided to move to a place called Ludlow, in Shropshire. They had longed to move from the hustle and bustle of the city. They liked the idea of the quiet countryside. So, Jane had found a job as a kennelmaid on a farm. They were provided with a nice cottage to live in, also, which came with the job.

The lady owner of the farm lived in a big farmhouse just down the road. She had many businesses and one of them was owning a boarding kennel for people who wanted to leave their dog while they went away on holiday.

Jane was paid a weekly salary and given accommodation, providing she fed the dogs and took care of their every whim. The accommodation was a quaint little two-bedroom, eighteenth-century cottage, complete with roses climbing up the wall beside the front door. They lived a peaceful and idyllic way of life. It was ideal for our John, who was now suffering with nervous tension. He yearned for peace and tranquillity, and the country cottage situated down a quiet country lane satisfied his needs.

John smoked a pipe. He would light up at regular intervals. He would say, 'It keeps me calm and focused.' It was good of Jane to find a job with a house so John needed not to worry about those things. At this time in his life, John was very delicate on the inside. Too many people around him would make him feel uneasy. The work he used to do, working as a butcher in a shop, he was unable to cope with now. So now John didn't have to worry at all about working the nine-to-five treadmill.

Occasionally, in the summer months, he would do a bit of labouring on the grand old lady's farm, like sheep-shearing or whatever. Just a little bit of general labour, from time to time.

He would often say to me, 'Just a bottle of beer and my pipe and I'm a happy man.'

I did visit him once or twice in the cottage. On the first occasion, he had felt sorry for a small whippet dog that had been abandoned. He had named the dog 'Blue'. They were companions and became inseparable

The cottage was tiny, made for small people, and our John was six-foot tall, so he had to duck when going from room to room. There was only one hearth, in a little lounge, where they would build a fire made from logs. They would make the fire in the evening to warm the house.

On the other hand, they were 'fresh air fiends'. Windows would be open while they slept at night, the bathroom window kept ajar all day and all night. The front door wouldn't be locked at all. Hardly anybody walked down the country lane. Their neighbourhood was safe to live in and their lives were minimal and simple. John and Jane were not materialistic people. They just loved the fresh air and the countryside and its rolling hills. The peace and quiet of the stillness is what they grew used to.

At night-time in bed, one could hear the night owls hooting in nearby woods, and listen to the occasional rustle in the hedgerow, now and again. Was it a fox or a badger...?

The dogs in the boarding kennel would occasionally bark. If one dog started to bark, then they would all join in until there was a chorus of high-pitched and deep-throated barking and howling. It was quite funny.

# Chapter Forty-Seven

It was around the year 1982. My sister had been reading the *Nottingham Evening Post*. In the personal column she found something interesting. There was a piece which read something like, 'Would anyone who knows June Glover or Marie Glover, please contact this number...' She realised one of the names was our mother's.

Well, surprised, she got into her car and drove down to my mother and father's house. She excitedly knocked on the door and my father opened it. On walking into the living room, she showed my mother the newspaper article that she had found. So, not knowing why the person had wanted to contact her, after a bit of discussion, my sister dialled the number.

A man's voice answered the phone. My sister explained that the woman he had wanted to contact was her mother and asked him what it was all about. The man introduced himself, then asked whether he could speak to June, so she handed the phone over.

Well, this amazing story unfolded. The man explained that his mother had just passed away. During her last days, she had mumbled about her two little girls. The man continued to say that after she died, he talked to a neighbour who was close to her. The neighbour had known she had abandoned two daughters when they were toddlers.

So this person on the other end of the phone was saying he was our mother's brother. And, if that wasn't enough of a surprise, he also went on to say that they had a sister too.

After quite a long conversation to verify all of the relatives' names and places visited, my mother invited him round to the house to meet the family. Well, this was extraordinary and so out of the blue.

The day came when this man arrived at the door. My mother and father sat listening intensely and discovered a whole new side to our family. The man had also produced some photographs and documents concerning his mother. The story unravelled.

It came to pass that the man—obviously younger than my mother—was called Derek. Apparently, his mother, Ethel May, had taken him away from her other two daughters when he was a tiny baby. She had run away to Spondon with her lover. Then later, she gave birth to a baby girl called Maisie. She was the lover's child, hence his half-sister. Baby Derek, when taken away, was my mum's full brother!

My mother and father must have sat there flabbergasted. I mean, of course, my mother had known she and her sister were abandoned and were brought up by their grandma—she had hardly ever seen her own mother during childhood.

But just imagine how my mother must have felt to discover her new brother. Later, she went on to meet her half-sister. What a surprise!

I should tell you about when I was a small girl, in the house, where Christopher died, the year was about 1964, a door-to-door salesman knocked on the door. He had sweeping brushes and all houseware stuff to sell. It turned out that he was my mum's dad, come to visit. Well, my mother, who was not well, at the time, argued with him and told him she didn't want to see him. She shouted at him and told him to go away.

I remember, as a child, the commotion at the back door, in the daytime when my father was out at work. My mother had called him 'Dad' and she wouldn't let him come into the house.

I also have a memory of going on a bus journey to a kind of hospital. There were long railings outside. It was in the summer. On putting two and two together, later, I think my mum visited her father in hospital, when he was ill and dying of cancer. On leaving the hospital, I remember my mother just casually said he'd died of cancer and there were no tears from her...

Also, there's another memory I have. When I was attending the local junior school, my mother had come to meet us from school, at the end of the school day. She would always come to meet us every day, as set in stone. On this occasion, an elderly lady, dressed in old fashioned clothes, was leaning against the school railings. She was looking at us children and talking to my mother. Indeed, I believe she was the long-lost mother, Ethel May. My mum spoke a few words, then told her to go away. But what I do remember, of Ethel May, is her kind, smiley face, I never saw her again.

So, you see, both parents had later come to look for their daughter. They had obviously found the neighbourhood where my mum had lived and knew she had children. Good detective work would find her at the local school. She had waited, at the end of the school day and worked out, which young woman, her daughter would be, I suppose.

It's very sad, I think, the whole story. If only my mother would have forgiven her, for running off. If only she had embraced her and welcomed her into her home. She could have forgiven her mother and father, for what they had done.

I always wonder what my grandmother's story might have been. My mother had obviously become bitter towards the very thought of her own mother. In fact, I still do not know my own mother's story, the story about her childhood, except I know there was poverty and hardship. I don't exactly know the details and I assume it wasn't very nice.

There was also poverty and hardship for Derek, her full brother and his half-sister, Maisie, as I learned when I took my mother to visit Derek later. He had apparently never married and lived with his mother until she died.

# Chapter Forty-Eight

Now my mother had new family members. She stayed in touch with her new brother, Derek, but only met the half-sister the one time.

At this time in my life, I was married and pregnant with my first baby. I took my mother over to Spondon in the car to visit Derek at his home. He lived in a semi-detached council house, where he greeted us at the door. We walked into the sparsely furnished lounge and sat down on the red settee. I looked around and noticed the window area. Am I seeing things? I thought. There were curtains hanging up. But on looking further, I could see they were hooked onto a cane, yes, a gardening cane. The cane, with curtain, was balanced on three nails hammered into the wooden batten above the window.

I do not know whether this was because of poverty or whether it was the eccentricity of my Uncle Derek. But thinking about it, he told us he had always worked for a living (in some obscure job) and that he had visited Australia to do some bird watching later on in his life. So, I think, as a working man and being able to save up enough money to fly long-haul to the other side of the world, he was probably quite 'well off' financially. It seemed perhaps he just chose to spend money carefully? Or was it because the house he lived in was his mother's house, so he didn't spend on it...? I think he was a bit of an eccentric character as, later, I was to find out.

Derek took us through to the kitchen and offered us a cup of tea. I noticed the oven was turned on and that the oven door was open. There was something laid out neatly on the oven shelf. To my surprise, I saw that it was in fact a pair of underpants! Derek saw that I noticed the pants and remarked, 'Oh yes, I use the oven to dry my clothes…'

We all returned to the red settee and talked mainly about his mother. When I asked questions about what sort of person she was, his answers were very guarded. He was protective about what he chose to reveal about her.

On hearing the whistle of the kettle and knowing it was boiling away on the stove, Derek walked back into the kitchen. He returned holding one mug of tea, which he offered to my mother. He explained I would have to wait for mine because he only had one mug in the house.

I had to chuckle to myself, as I realised, in fact, he *was* one of life's eccentrics. My mother just ignored him and carried on talking as she turned the pages of an old photograph album. A picture of her mother was taken out by Derek and given to her, to keep for herself.

The visit was short. We walked out of the house through the back door. I noticed the tidy garden. Tall flowers were grown. Flowers such as Sweet William, delphiniums and lupins were neatly supported, in rows, by canes. My mother and I bid farewell and went home.

Derek later made subsequent visits to my mother and father's home. The last time we heard of him was when he had been taken into a care home, where he later passed away.

# Chapter Forty-Nine

My dear father had offered to help me decorate a small room in my house where I lived with my husband. It was quite rare for my dad to visit any family members really. Although at this point in time, we had a good relationship.

He pulled up in his car outside my house. I happened to live nearby in the Carlton area of Nottingham, near to the family home. It was mid-morning time of day. I showed my dad the room that I wanted to be papering—just one wall. He proceeded to get his tools of the trade out of a small box. My father worked quickly and neatly. He finished the job and I was pleased with the result.

I switched on the electric kettle to make a cup of tea. We sat down at the dining room table and drank it together. While in conversation, he started to criticise my elder sister. You see, reader, my sister was recently divorced. She had run off with another man and left her children with her husband. My father really laid into the fact that she had committed adultery and was therefore a bad person. He rambled on and on, decimating her character. I hadn't the patience to listen to his ongoing tirade, nor was I in the mood to listen, so I flipped.

'Dad, that's my sister you're talking about. I don't like the things you are saying!'

Standing up from the table, I told him to go, for I did not want to hear any more.

He stood up from his chair and said, 'Right, I will go now and I'm never coming back!'

That was it. I watched him walk down the path, get into his car and speed off. And I will tell you, true to his word, he never ever visited my house again...

A few weeks later—after letting the dust settle—I went over to visit my parents. My mother opened the door and said, 'Your dad doesn't want to see you.'

Well, this really hurt my feelings. I understood how he must have been hurt by what I had said, but surely, he should understand why. I thought families should support each other and not bad-mouth one another as my father had done. He didn't understand that he was talking about my sister, whom I was close to, in a derogatory way.

Anyway, I walked warily into the living room where Dad was sitting in his chair. I said I was sorry for what happened. I apologised profusely. It was like treading on eggshells... and the stilted conversation which followed was rather awkward. You see, reader, in Jamaican culture, one is supposed to respect one's elders by not answering back and making your opinion known. A child should accept the wishes of their father and mother, who know best. In my father's eyes, I had been totally disrespectful to him in the way I asked him to leave my house. But this is where the two cultures clash. I was brought up the English way because I live in England... but my father was Jamaican...

After my apology, which he accepted, he said he still would not enter my house ever again. Dad was stubborn and rigid. He would never relent on anything he said and believed in. Always stubborn and true to his word.

# Chapter Fifty

We four daughters were marrying and having children of our own. My mother and father were enjoying their grandchildren, who visited the house regularly. My father was heading towards retiring from Boots in a few years.

At work, Dad was asked to attend an 'anger management' course. Oh dear, reader, you are probably asking, 'Ooh, what has happened this time?' Ha! I smile...

Well, what had occurred on his way to work one morning I will tell you...

My father had just 'pulled up' in his car to wait at the barrier to enter his workplace car park. The person in front was delaying the flow of traffic in my father's eyes, messing about and being stupid. My dad got out of his car and walked over to 'have a word' with the driver. The person also ventured to open his car door and walked behind to 'have a word' with my father. Words were spoken, and a fight broke out. The man said something like, 'Do not mess with me 'cos I'm a judo expert.' And my dad was flung to the ground, hurting his shoulder.

Do you know, reader, he continued to stay at work until the pain in his shoulder became unbearable. At lunchtime, realising there was something radically wrong, he decided to drive himself home. On discussion with Mum, he proceeded to take himself off to the accident and emergency department, at the local hospital. It was discovered he had dislocated his shoulder blade. The judo expert had 'done him in' good and proper.

The incident was recorded by the gate staff and reported to the senior management team. So later, my father was called to a meeting regarding the altercation where he was asked to attend an anger management course.

My father had always been an angry person from as far back as I can remember. He had a short fuse. All through my childhood, his temper was always just bubbling beneath the surface. It mellowed, a little bit, in later years. It is a known trait in Mediterranean people—referring to his mother's side of the family—for being quick-tempered and fiery. I suppose a few will escape this stereotype.

# Chapter Fifty-One

My father's retirement day came in the summer of his sixty-fifth birthday. A lifetime of work was to come to an end. When employees at Boots the chemist retired, the management always arranged a little party with their colleagues, and family was invited also.

The reason why my father had come to England from Jamaica was solely to be able to join a workforce. He wanted to be able to show his wealth by sending money home: to his mother and father, sisters and brother. He would have been so proud to do this and show his family he left behind that he could indeed make something of himself in the Mother Country.

He had fulfilled his dream, for if he had stayed in his homeland, he would have probably taken over from his father the cultivation of fruits and vegetables on the land. His life would not have been the same. He would have grown his own crops, cared for his own chickens, goats and donkey. He would have 'lived off the land' and sold a bit of produce at the market in Saint Ann, occasionally, for a bit of cash. His own brother had worked at the bauxite mine for a while and then the work dried up. Jobs were fickle, fought over and far between.

My father never travelled back to Jamaica, unfortunately. He wrote frequently, to his sisters and brother. Letters and Christmas cards were exchanged throughout his life. When he retired, long distance, lengthy phone calls became a normal part of his everyday life....

Now it was the time for his retirement. He sighed and sat back in his comfortable armchair and must have thought, 'Yes, it was truly worth it... leaving my homeland.'

Anyway, my father asked for us four daughters to attend his retirement party. It was to be held one afternoon at his workplace. Only our mother attended. This was because his daughters were working and too busy looking after children. He was awarded the proverbial clock and some garden chairs. He celebrated with workmates and managers. Photographs were taken by a Boots photographer to mark the occasion.

So that was it. My father had officially retired. He told me that he was glad and that he could do more gardening.

He decided to sell his car, because he had not needed to go anywhere in it. My mother had also refused to travel anywhere in the car with him at the wheel. Smile...

My younger sister was still living at home, but otherwise Mum and Dad were free agents. Free to do anything they wished or go anywhere they wanted. But they weren't travellers, nor had they ever been on foreign holidays. I would say the majority of their generation were stay-at-home people. One would say they were just homely people.

# Chapter Fifty-Two

In retirement, my father generally enjoyed good health. He was of slim build and spritely. Although there was a slight hiccup in his health when he went to the hospital for investigations of his heart rhythms. His heart had been beating sometimes fast, sometimes intermittently. He was prescribed some tablets and the matter resolved itself.

Healthwise, he was now fine and sailed through into his seventies. Anyway, things were going okay for my dad but not so well for his troubled son John. Brace yourself, reader, for what I'm about to tell you...

In January 1991, his eldest son, John, seemed to have committed suicide. I say 'seemed' because there was an inquest and the cause of death was undecided. The coroner declared an 'open verdict'. My second brother had taken his own life. I will explain the sequence of events.

Around Christmas 1990, my brother John had phoned my father to say he was coming home to live because he had 'split up' with his wife, Jane. He subsequently had hired a car and drove from Shropshire to Nottingham. He arrived at my mother and father's home with a bag packed with clothes and a few belongings. Apparently, Jane had been having an affair with a military man. She was working as his housekeeper. He'd owned a substantial house in the rolling countryside and was quite wealthy.

John had accepted this and seemed eager to 'move on' and make a fresh start in his life. (They had no children in the marriage.) Knowing he had elderly parents with a home with two spare bedrooms, John easily assumed his place in the family home.

Christmas was approaching. John was trying to make a new life in Nottingham. He remembered the name of an old school friend. Thumbing through the telephone directory (a thick, chunky book, full of names, addresses and telephone numbers, which was usually placed under the home landline telephone for convenience), he came across the name and phone number of his old school friend. Dialling the number, the voice on the other end said hello. The man remembered John and they started to chat. The conversation ended with the man saying he was too busy with his family commitments and was unable to meet up with John. So, disappointed, John accepted this. He would visit his sister, who lived in the city with her partner. There, they would smoke joints of marijuana. He would stay with them until the early hours of the morning, then slope off home. His visits became all too frequent and his sister became annoyed. They had 'had words' and fallen out.

So John was cooped up in the family home with only his mother and father for companionship. They were now older, quiet people, who hardly socialised. Christmas was just around the corner and John had asked his father to accompany him to the local pub to have a few drinks. His father refused, said he didn't enjoy pubs.

Now, John had an old friend he had known when he lived in Birmingham. Apparently, they had been very close at one time. John told me they had many adventures together and were like brothers. His name was Rupert, 'Rupe' for short. He phoned him and had a chat, then asked Dad whether Rupe could come over and stay for a few days. Dad's answer was no because he didn't know the guy.

So previously John had been known to have smuggled a friend into his bedroom without father knowing...

John had been down to the JobCentre to try to sort out some kind of work. For a few weeks he went to work in an abattoir in Nottingham. He was, after all, a qualified butcher from all those years ago when he had worked in the supermarket. It was only temporary work for the Christmas period. The job quickly came to an end.

So off he went down to the Jobcentre again to try to find something more permanent. He came home and talked about the North Sea oil rigs, which needed workers in the New Year.

In fact, as a Christmas present, I had bought him some thermal long johns with matching vest, ready to take to the oil rigs. Christmas Day came and went. John had had a phone call from friends in Shropshire and decided to drive down there in the New Year to tie up some loose ends. So, after the celebrations, he decided to hire a car and off he went. Something had upset him and while returning home to his mother and father, he had crashed the hire car. The wing was badly damaged, but he managed to drive back.

On returning to the family home, John was clearly deeply troubled. He had a confused mind. I don't know whether he had been taking his tablets for his mental health issues, or not. He was emotionally unbalanced, according to other family members. This was not a good way to be for a person like John.

It isn't clear how he had crashed the car. Had he accidently run into a wall... Crashed into another car, bus, lorry or worse? John had very little to say about what had actually happened.

It was a very dark January. The evenings were cold and gloomy. This particular January, I remember there were very high winds. Fences rattled and trees were bent over. It was dark, stormy and cold. Very little snow, though.

On a Sunday afternoon at the family home, John had retired to his bedroom. He always liked to read novels or motoring magazines, so there was nothing unusual about him taking to his room. After about half an hour, my parents heard an almighty 'thud'—like someone or something had fallen to the floor. Immediately, my father walked rapidly up the stairs to investigate.

He knocked on John's door and walked in, asking whether everything was alright. On entering, he saw John slumped back on his bed. There was a pool of blood and more was pumping out of his groin area. There was a knife on the bed. My father managed to grab an item of nearby clothing and packed it tightly into his body to stem the flow. He then shouted downstairs to Mum to call for an ambulance. The ambulance arrived and they tried to save his life in the bedroom. After they tidied him up, they took him to hospital.

In the meantime, my father had telephoned me at my house to say that John had been taken to hospital. He said he had cut himself and added that he thought he wouldn't live...

I rushed round to the house where, one by one, all three sisters arrived. There was a policewoman standing guard at the front door. A police detective was already inside the house, talking to my parents. As I started to venture up the stairs—for nobody had told me the finer details about what had happened—the detective stepped forward and advised, 'I wouldn't go up there if I was you,' giving me an ominous look.

In the lounge, Dad told us girls about what had happened, the knife and all that. I remember the telephone ringing in the hallway—by then I was in the dining room. The police detective answered the call. 'Oh, okay,' he said, then replaced the handset in the receiver. He turned to us all and said, 'I'm sorry, he's died. That was the hospital...'

We all cried and wept uncontrollably.

After a while, us sisters 'pulled ourselves together'. We decided to go and visit John at the hospital. The detective informed them of our imminent arrival.

Weeks later, there was an inquest into his death. They wanted a statement from my father and I was asked to testify regarding John's state of mind. I had said that he was planning for the future and he was going to work on the oil rigs in the North Sea, starting in the New Year. After hearing all of the evidence, the judge decided to grant an 'open verdict' as to the cause of his death.

# Chapter Fifty-Three

After John's death, my father remained strong, but I feel he was in shock. In fact, the whole family was in a state of surrealism, thinking, 'Did this really happen?' or 'Am I dreaming? I think my father was just stunned for the first year or so.

Dad immersed himself in his gardening. Mowing the lawn was his solace. He took great pride in trimming the lawn edges to immaculate perfection. He reorganised the garden. He rearranged flower beds. The garden became even more his work of art, his jewel, his passion.

He paid tree surgeons to shape his conifers. The huge weeping willow tree at the back of the house was trimmed to a more manageable size. Many a time, after spending all day in the outdoors, he would sit and relax in his armchair to admire the view. Everything neat and tidy.

Peace and quiet. This is what my father enjoyed at this stage in his life. In his retirement, he would walk to the local library to fetch a few novels to read. He liked crime novels and Cowboy and Indian type books, the occasional autobiography. Often, he would walk into Arnold to pay his Council Tax bill, in an office that was situated in the grounds of Arnot Hill Park. He enjoyed the fresh air and the walk through the park. He preferred to walk and would hardly ever take the bus.

He liked to watch political news items on the television. Occasionally, he would cook one of his famous West Indian dinners. He would fry some chicken with onions, chilli peppers and a blend of curry spices with tomatoes. He would cook a pot of rice and peas. In a frying pan, there would be his cheesecakes and dumplings sizzling away. My father was a good cook.

My mother and father wouldn't take any holidays anymore. They were home birds. Quite contented with just the family visiting often. There were even more grandchildren now. The family was still growing and became more interesting to them. There was always lots to talk about.

The days were more or less the same. Like a lot of elderly couples of their generation, they socialised less frequently and preferred the peacefulness of their own home.

The years passed by until 1999 turned into the year 2000, the Millennium year. As you can imagine, there were huge celebrations taking place all over the world. This marked the end of the 90s and the start of the 2000s.

At the time in the media there was talk of a computer bug, known as the Y2K bug. Because of the zeros in 2000, it was thought the many computerised establishments, finance, business and commerce would not be able to handle all the zeros in digital form. So they were concerned as to what would actually happen when the date on their computers changed to the year 2000. In fact, this turned out not to be true. Computerised systems managed the change successfully.

So, the people and the world at the time experienced a sense of mild panic. The year 2000 was regarded as being futuristic, perhaps being seen as a Utopian kind of world. On this particular New Year's Eve, there were parties and celebrations enough to beat all previous. Even folk who did not usually celebrate New Year just had to come out of their houses to enjoy the state of euphoria that most were feeling. A new era was formed.

Though there were global celebrations, it was argued that the celebrations for the Millennium should have been a year later—1 January 2001. Scientists debated over the true date of the third millennium. Some respected scientific institutions such as the Royal Greenwich Observatory insisted the start of the twenty-first century should be marked and celebrated on 1 January 2001. The *Encyclopædia Britannia* also agreed and stood by this as the truth.

# Chapter Fifty-Four

In the March of the year 2000, my mother died. She was 72 years old. She had been a heavy smoker all of her life. One day, at the family home, she had felt ill, so she had taken herself to bed. This was unusual for Mum, because even if she had felt ill before, she would just sit in her armchair and rest her head on the arm of the chair.

The next day, she decided to get herself dressed and venture downstairs into the living room where she sat in her armchair. My father said she looked really ill in her face and her breathing was far from good. He decided to phone the doctor's surgery to summon the doctor over to the house.

After lunchtime, the doctor arrived. On examining her, he said she'd got a chest infection and wrote out a prescription for an antibiotic medicine. Swiftly, father walked up to Mapperley Plains to the chemist shop and brought home the medication.

She took one antibiotic tablet, with a glass of water as prescribed. About half an hour later, she got up out of her armchair and walked into the front dining room. She sat down on a dining chair and gazed out of the window. My father was busy upstairs, tidying up or something. He came downstairs and asked her how she was feeling. Not saying a word, my mother stood up from her chair and lay down on the carpeted floor. She folded her arms over her chest and passed away.

He knelt beside her, shouting, 'Juney, Juney.' He soon realised she had died. He decided to pick her up and move her to the settee in the living room, thinking it was undignified being stretched out on the floor. She had always been a thin woman, but she was tall, and he struggled to move her.

This was the account my father had told me, for I never knew she had fallen ill. I hadn't been round to visit for a few weeks.

I had had a phone call later that afternoon from my sister, who told me to come over to the house because our mother had died. She said she had rung my house about five times previously, but I had gone out to do some shopping. So when I did pick up the phone, she was frantic and just burst out telling me the dreadful news. Ironically, while out, I had bought a Mother's Day card...

On arriving at the house, I entered the lounge. There, I found my mother stretched out on the settee, as if sleeping. Sooner than later, all sisters arrived. We cried buckets of tears and so did Father. It was a sudden death. None of us knew she was that ill. Only a day or two of feeling unwell, then gone. Gone from this earth.

My father arranged the funeral. He remained strong. We all decided on a cremation because that's what our mother had wished, then the ashes were to be buried in Christopher's grave.

I remember the vicar was present at the graveside to say a few words. All the family was gathered around. Then my father gently lifted the prearranged sod of earth. Tears rolling down his face, he gently placed her ashes into the ground.

# Chapter Fifty-Five

Approximately nine months later, after Mum had passed away, a little girl was born into the family. Isn't it strange? One person dies then is replaced, almost immediately, by another. I suspected I was expecting a baby at the time of my mother's funeral. My baby girl was born in the November.

I visited my father often during the lead up to the baby's birth. Father was coping okay on his own. The new baby in the family brought him joy—and I suppose 'hope'. Hope in the way that there was indeed a future.

The first Christmas after Mother's death was joyous but tinged with sadness. The new baby was the centre of attention at the family gathering. The crying of the poor little mite brought smiles to people's faces.

I brought the baby to Dad's house frequently as a distraction following the bereavement. He played with her and generally looked after her, from time to time. All was well.

Father was interested in politics and world affairs. He would watch programmes on the television in the comfort of his own home. He would follow the news and buy newspapers regularly. Also, he still liked the gee-gees, as in horse racing.

Often, he would walk to Arnold to have his hair cut at a barber's shop across from Arnot Hill Park. He would walk up to the Co-op to buy his groceries. Walking was Dad's passion. He had walked across fields back home in Jamaica as a child.

His memories of walking to his grandma's house every morning to fetch the milk stayed with him.

Always at six o'clock sharp in the evening, he would cook a meal for himself. He wasn't the kind of person to eat ready-prepared supermarket meals. He would always cook from scratch. In fact, I do not believe he had ever eaten a Chinese takeaway or an Indian meal—for that matter, any pre-cooked meal.

Dad was a stickler for routine. Perhaps because of his RAF training. Always on a Monday, he would wash his own clothes in the washing machine, then hang them to dry on his clothes horse, which was kept in the spare bedroom. Midweek, he would hoover the carpets and keep the home as clean and tidy as he could. He would eat lunch at one o'clock sharp—he would check his wrist-watch. When he saw it was approaching six o'clock, then he would start to prepare his evening meal.

He had plenty of time to potter about his garden, mowing the lawn and neatening the edges. Rose bushes were clipped and pruned at the appropriate time of year. He even dug a small vegetable patch at the side of the patio—only growing rhubarb in it though.

Smile.

Often time, small saplings and various plants would suddenly spring up in his garden. My father had not planted them there. This was because where the house was built previously, there had been a small wooded area. People from neighbouring houses would dump their garden waste in the wood. So years later, plants would suddenly shoot up all over our garden. For example, bluebells and small holly saplings would show in the springtime.

When any of us sisters visited, he would ask us whether we wanted any plants for our garden, the bluebells or suchlike. He would then dig them up, wrap them in newspaper and then present them to us. He would also divide his tulip bulbs and give them to us in the same way. Dad filled his time and had plenty of visits from family members.

# Chapter Fifty-Six

The years rolled by. My father still generally enjoyed good health, though his mobility started to slow him down. It was round about the year 2006 when my father was diagnosed with arthritis. He had been developing aches and pains for a while, but the pain was more particularly evident in his right knee. The intensity of the pain varied according to the weather. (Some types of arthritis become more painful in colder weather. The barometric pressure can affect sufferers also.)

On visiting Dad, I would ask him how he was. He would say, 'Oh, the old knee, a bit of pain.' Even later, when he was in excruciating pain, he would bear it by taking a paracetamol or two. He would just say, 'It's the Lord's wish…' He wouldn't make a song and dance about the pain. I would look over to glance at him. I knew he was suffering, but he wouldn't complain much at all. He just kept it to himself.

My sister took him to the doctor's surgery, where he was hobbling and holding onto furniture. He was advised to seek assistance from the occupational health team. They would make a visit to his home to assess his everyday living requirements. For example, whether he was able to rise from his armchair comfortably. Or did he need his chair made higher for him to be able to get out of it more easily? Dad was soon assessed and given a walking stick to use. His knee was beginning to stiffen up and he was soon unable to bear weight on it.

The whole house was assessed. His bed was lifted onto wooden blocks to make it easier to get in and out. A high frame was put around the toilet, for the same reasons. Dad was fine though, accepting his new incapabilities.

One day, all us sisters were visiting, as usual with our children. We had a conversation about Dad struggling to get up the stairs, to bed or to use the toilet, which was upstairs. He had found out the cost of a stairlift and was horrified. The one he thought about buying was priced at £6,000. He was worried about the heavy cost. Although Father could easily afford it, having thousands stashed away in the bank from a lump sum of money given to him on his retirement, he seemed reluctant to spend it.

He asked us daughters to give our opinion. We all agreed that if he needed to buy a stairlift, he should do so and not worry about the cost. My Father had worked hard all of his life and could spend his money however he wished.

So, Monday morning, first thing, he got on the phone and asked the salesman to come round to the house to measure up and advise. The stairlift was installed quickly.

When all of us sisters visited the next time, we each took it in turns to 'have a go'. Even grandchildren all had a ride up the stairs—and down again—on Grandad's stairlift!

The heartbreaking thing about the loss of his mobility was that he was unable to mow his beloved lawn anymore. Oh, the look of sadness overwhelmed his face at the sheer reality of his situation.

Dad was using the stairlift successfully. I once visited him on a warm sunny day. He had attempted to venture out of his lounge patio door and into the garden. He was stuck. He couldn't get himself back into the house. The back step was too high for him to lift his leg up onto the step. He found it difficult to put pressure on his good leg, to enable him to get himself back inside.

Ha! Ha! He was laughing. I said something like, 'Dad, what are you like!'

He thought it was hilarious being stuck out in the garden like a stupid old goat. He explained that he was just looking out of the window and thought, 'If only I could just tidy up that rose bush out there; it's annoying me. I got my clippers okay from the kitchen drawer. Got outside and trimmed it. But then… it's that step. Too high…'

We both laughed as I helped him up into the house. It was a bit difficult. He had to sit on the step on his backside then swing his legs onto the lounge carpet. With my help and his walking stick he was able to stand upright. I gently reprimanded him and said, 'What if it started to rain and nobody was around to help you? You would be soaking wet!'

Later, he just accepted he was housebound and nothing like it ever happened again. He employed an occasional gardener, just to mow the lawn and generally tidy up to keep the weeds at bay.

# Chapter Fifty-Seven

My father had always followed politics and world affairs. Watching the news one day, he was mesmerised by hearing a speech from an American called Barack Obama. Obama was running to be leader of the Democratic Party. In the final round he was up against a woman called Hillary Clinton. This guy was a campaigner for equal rights and had focused his attention on the poor people of Chicago—for there was a lot of poverty and hopelessness for black Americans. Obama campaigned for criminal justice for the unfairly treated minorities. On 3 January 2008, he won a surprise victory in Iowa over Hillary Clinton, who had been the favourite to win.

They continued to campaign in different states. His speeches were now being broadcast in the United Kingdom and indeed all over the world. Obama had won over more American states than Hillary Clinton. Finally, he succeeded overall and became the new leader of the Democratic Party.

Special programmes were being broadcast all over British television. My father would sit and watch in awe at Obama's oratory and stirring speeches. He was inspirational and moved the listener. Obama had charisma and style. People liked him. Son of a Kenyan father and a white woman, he was truly a light in this unpredictable world. People began to take notice of this man.

Whenever I visited my dad, we would always speak about Barack Obama. 'Did you hear the speech in New Hampshire, yesterday? Oh, the man can talk and is highly intelligent,' my father would exclaim.

He'd read all about Obama in the newspapers. He devoured every ounce of information about the guy. So, when I visited, we would discuss him at great length. Politics excited my father.

Obama appeared on many campaign stages and would draw the crowds in with his great personality and well written speeches. He was all over the British newspapers and news stations. Nobody had seen or heard a man of colour speak so eloquently since Martin Luther King. Well, now there was going to be a general election to vote for a new President of the United States of America. Obama was leader of the Democratic Party. John McCain led the Republican Party. Many speeches were made, these men challenging each other. McCain was stating that Obama was too inexperienced for the presidency. The final stages were to be run to decide who was going to become the new president.

My father gasped, 'Oh my, oh my. A black man to win the presidency? It is truly amazing. After all the slavery and history that's gone on before. I can see it though. Obama is good.'

In the January of the year 2009, Barack Obama did become the President of the United States of America. The first African American President in history. Thousands of people had turned out on the streets in the cold weather of Washington DC. Barack Obama was to be seen taking the oath of office.

All us sisters and our dad watched this great historical event broadcast all over the world, on our televisions. My father watched his television morning, noon and night. The inauguration was repeated on different channels. He was in awe of Barack Obama.

JULIE WOOD

'Oh my! I can't believe it. In a country like America and the way they treated black people in slavery, it is truly amazing. How society has changed over the years! When I came over from Jamaica in the war, it was such a different story. I have seen the changes here, the acceptance of the black man. Although there is still bigotry, but it is more hidden now. It is more subtle these days.'

# Chapter Fifty-Eight

Around the year 2010, my father had bouts of being ill. He was admitted to hospital on several occasions, mainly for infections. I lived close to his house, so he would always telephone when he was feeling unwell. My father was now well into his eighties and quite frail. He could still walk around the house with the aid of a walking stick—never a Zimmer frame. One had been delivered to the house, but he had refused to use it. So it just stood hidden away in the back bedroom.

Smile.

You see, my dad was still a proud man who wanted to walk as upright as he could. Being ex- RAF military man right up to the end, I suppose. He would still cook his evening meal at six o'clock sharp, hobbling, with his walking stick, into the kitchen. Sometimes, he would make enough dinner to last two days. Eat one plate and save the rest for the next day so just warming it up. 'A warm-up job tonight,' he would say.

One day, he found he had a waterworks problem. The doctor was called and Dad was advised to go to hospital in his own time. I would take him myself in the car. Investigations took place. He would be given a load of tablets then sent home as quickly as possible. There was a shortage of hospital beds.

I would take him home in the car, then look after him, with the help of my sisters, in his home. The district nurse would pop in from time to time. My father was now taking several tablets per day. I think I had counted ten in total!

So, over the next few years, in and out of hospital, nothing that serious. Each time—about four or five times—Dad made a full recovery. I'm glad my dad was able to walk around his home, albeit with the aid of a walking stick. He was always fine, of sound mind also, sharp as a razor. His memory was indeed better than mine, especially when remembering what had happened the week before.

I recall one occasion. It was at the weekend. I was at home and my telephone rang in the morning. It was my dad. 'Jules, I can hardly breathe. I have phoned for an ambulance and have opened the front door.'

'Okay, Dad, I'm coming round.'

On arriving at my father's house, the ambulance was already parked outside. On entering the house, Dad was seated in his armchair. An oxygen mask had been placed over his nose and mouth. He was visibly gasping for air. I identified myself as his daughter. The paramedics had said they had found him in the hallway, on the floor, gasping for air. They encouraged him to take deep breaths and to try to relax.

They had escorted him into an armchair. Blood pressure checks had been made, also his pulse taken. The paramedics explained he needed to go to hospital. I could see that Dad was stable, so I followed the ambulance in my own car. I contacted my sisters to let them know and locked up the house behind me.

In the casualty area, I found my father lying in a hospital bed, propped up by pillows. I took his hand and asked him how he felt. He nodded his head, as the mask was obstructing his mouth. Then a few tears fell from his eyes. I glanced at my father and saw that he was frightened. My eyes filled with water and he saw my tears.

Quickly, I fetched some tissues and wiped his eyes, then my own. No words had been spoken, but we fully understood each other. My father stayed in hospital for a couple of days, for there was no infection. I went to collect him to take him home. Again, he was given even more tablets. Some medication had been changed. After discharge from hospital, the district nurse visited frequently to monitor his progress.

Dad was admitted to hospital again six months later, this time for an infection. But each time he went in, there was panic inside of me. Will he come out again? It was always a worry.

Dad was well looked after at home. Remember, he had four daughters. I would do the shopping, mostly at the weekend. I would also organise medical appointments. My sister would wash his clothes and bedding using the automatic washing machine; another sister, who had two boys would trim his hair. Another sister had stayed away for reasons unknown. Plenty of grown-up grandchildren visited from time to time. For he was a well-loved and well-respected grandfather and great-grandfather.

I noticed, in about the year 2013, that his legs were becoming a little weaker. I was talking to him and he muttered something about getting up in the night to use the toilet and falling onto the floor. He said he felt too weak to stand up and had to pull the duvet off the bed to cover himself to keep himself warm until the morning. He didn't really make a meal of what had happened. But I suspected this was now becoming a common occurrence. Once, I went upstairs to find his bedside table upturned and the lamp askew on the floor.

It was now Christmastime. The family visited all over Christmas. Dad was well cared for and looked after. Then suddenly, in between Christmas and the New Year, my father developed a cold, a sore throat, sneezing and all that. He took the cold remedies and they seemed to help. New Year's Day came. We all telephoned him—as we always did—to wish him a happy New Year.

Then the next day, my father telephoned me. I could hear his voice, much deeper, and a rasping, wheezing sound. He said he felt unwell and would I come over. On opening the door with my key, I could hear his rattling, rasping. He was sitting in his armchair in the lounge. Every time he spoke, his chest rattled. So I now realised the cold had spread to his chest.

I phoned the surgery, and a doctor came round to the house within the hour. Dad was upbeat talking to her. She was jollying him along asking his age, 'Oh, ninety-one, never! You look much younger,' she would say. She checked the usual things, like blood pressure and heartbeat. She then asked me to venture outside to her assistant's car to ask for an oxygen meter. I swiftly did this and came back. The oxygen reading was a little on the low side.

She suggested Dad should go to hospital, 'Shall I arrange for an ambulance to take him? Or perhaps you would like to use your car, in your own time?' she said.

I replied, 'I will take him.'

After the doctor had left the house, I opened the cupboard door to fetch his overcoat. On seeing it, he said, 'No, I think I'll have my dressing gown.' His chest was rattling even more. It didn't sound good to me. I knew in my heart if he'd developed pneumonia, he was a gonner.

I helped him tighten his dressing gown belt. On checking the house was safe and adjusting the dial on the heating system, I locked up and helped him into my car.

The casualty area was very full. My father sat down on a chair and waited. I went over to the desk and checked Dad in. I asked the nurse for some oxygen, as Dad was gasping for breath. Another person came over and placed a mask over his nose and mouth area, the tube attached to an oxygen cylinder. Soon my father was wheeled into a consultation room. I had phoned my sisters and they appeared one by one. The consultant doctor assisted him onto a bed. I asked, 'How do you feel, Dad?'

He replied, 'I feel lousy.' They wheeled him off onto a ward.

Over the next few days, the grandchildren visited. There was always a family member by his side, day and night.

On the Saturday, a few days after being admitted, my father passed away.

It was the fourth of January 2014.

A true story about a Jamaican man, who travelled to England, during the Second World War. He had been recruited into the British Royal Air Force, on the island of Jamaica. I trace his journey and how it was.

After a while, he left the military and settled in Nottingham. There, he found work as a coal miner.

I tell the story of his life through the decades, until the year 2014, when he passed away.

Life for him wasn't all rosy.

Prejudices of the British people...

The sudden death of his five year old son...

The slow decline of his wife's mental health, was apparent, leaving her hospitalised...

His family were left homeless, when a business venture went awry...

In his final years, he was able to live in a beautiful, peaceful neighbourhood, but tragedy reared it's ugly head again.

ISBN 978-1-83615-235-4

9 781836 152354

90000